CD
INCLUDED

Guitar Explorer

A GUITARIST'S GUIDE TO
THE STYLES AND TECHNIQUES OF ETHNIC
INSTRUMENTS FROM AROUND THE WORLD

BY GREG HERRIGES

T0081545

ISBN 978-1-4234-2356-0

HAL•LEONARD®
CORPORATION

7777 W. BLUEMOUND RD. P.O. BOX 13819 MILWAUKEE, WI 53213

In Australia Contact:
Hal Leonard Australia Pty. Ltd
4 Lentara Court
Cheltenham, Victoria, 3192 Australia
Email: ausadmin@halleonard.com.au

Visit Hal Leonard Online at
www.halleonard.com

Preface

What do all the great pioneers of the guitar have in common? They weren't just following in other guitarists' footsteps! Charlie Christian played horn licks on the electric guitar. Jimi Hendrix learned a lot from the Indian veena. Chet Atkins' virtuoso picking was more than a little bit banjo-inspired. In a world full of great guitar players who know each other's licks inside and out, how do you set yourself apart and draw new inspiration for your music? By looking beyond your instrument and your boundaries.

In exploring the styles and techniques of *non-guitar* instruments from around the world, the lessons in this book/CD will help change your way of thinking not only about the guitar as an instrument, but also about the way music is put together. The balalaika, the shamisen, and the mbira are not just ethnic instruments; they're vehicles for different kinds of expression from different traditions on different continents. You'll learn to manipulate six strings in ways that you might not be used to, and whether you're looking to enhance your playing with new sounds and techniques, find new composing tools, or develop a world music repertoire, you'll have a better understanding of what makes each tradition—and technique—unique.

The research, writing, and recording that went into this volume have been a great opportunity for me to explore new horizons as a guitarist. I hope the discoveries are as rewarding for you as the journey has been for me!

Acknowledgments

Thanks to all the entities and organisms that made this project possible, including but not limited to:

- New Folk Records
- The Bush Foundation
- Indian Music Society of Minnesota (IMSOM)
- All at Hal Leonard Corporation
- All other donors of images, skills, and knowledge (listed within)

CD Credits

Greg Herriges: guitars

Marc Anderson: tabla, percussion

All tracks Recorded by John Wright at The Villa, Savage, MN, except track 3, recorded at Hamline University Studio, St. Paul, MN

Mixed by John Wright at The Villa

CONTENTS

INTRODUCTION

Your first requirement is to stop being a guitar player. No, don't throw away the prized instrument that has brought meaning and adoring fans into your life! Just start approaching it in new ways. Most of us guitarheads have spent our formative years (in our parents' basements) learning how to strum, arpeggiate, riff, and pick within proper chord progressions, exactly like the hallowed six-string fretted-neck pioneers who came before us to establish the templates from which we've been stamped. And why not? It is satisfying to learn every nuance of a legendary guitarist's licks and facial ticks. But now that you've developed great chops and imitative skills, it's time for a new challenge: to use those skills to learn phrases and styles from other musical languages. When those exotic sounds and tonalities mix with your own guitar mastery, you'll have the tools to adapt, fuse, and build a style that is all your own.

Elements of World Music

It's impossible to categorize all music, but it is important to know what distinguishes some traditions from others, especially if you want to learn to play in many styles.

Some general distinctions can be made between traditional music of the West (including Europe and the North and South Americas) and that of the East (including India, the Middle East, and much of East Asia). There are many exceptions to all of this, but here is a snapshot comparison:

IN THE WEST:	IN THE EAST:
Melody happens over **harmony** (*chord progressions*).	Melody often happens over a **drone** (real or implied).
Melody comes first and its delivery is subjective.	Melodic **ornaments** are important and sometimes strict.
Four- and three-beat cycles are standard.	Beat cycles vary (and are often **odd**).
The emphasis is on **melody** (percussion is mostly supportive).	**Melody** and **rhythm** are equally important.
Tunes are usually **pre-composed**.	There is more emphasis on **improvisation**.

Here is a little more explanation of some of the concepts above:

The Drone – a real or implied tonic note (or chord) that underlies the entire piece of music, rather than a chord progression.

"Odd" Time Signatures – music grouped in sets of five, seven, thirteen, and other beat cycles that might feel "uneven" compared to most even-numbered Western time signatures.

Ornaments – in the West, we first learn to sing or play a melody *straight*, i.e., without grace notes, vibrato, etc., and when we do add embellishments, they are usually at the performer's discretion. In much of the East, the ornaments are built into the melody from the start and are just as important as the main melody notes. You'll also find that it's the style of ornamentation that really makes your playing sound "Indian," "African," "Middle Eastern," and so on.

HOW TO USE THIS BOOK/CD

The lessons in this book are geared toward intermediate and advanced guitar players, but relative beginners and non-guitarists will benefit from it as well. In fact, a "less advanced" player might have the advantage of fewer preconceived notions on how the guitar should be played, and therefore an easier time adapting to some of the craziest techniques in the book. Having said that, the lessons assume that you:

- read tablature and/or standard music notation;

- have a basic knowledge of chords, scales, and intervals;

- are comfortable with chord strumming, single-note picking, and some fingerstyle playing;

- have an open mind and an appetite for new ways of making music.

Lessons are not ordered according to difficulty, so feel free to skip around the book and find the styles that suit your level of expertise or interest.

What You Will Need:

- Steel- or nylon-string acoustic guitar (ideally, both!)

- Capo

- Fingers and a pick

- Optional tools listed within (e.g., staples and spare change)

In our Western European musical terms, we can say that each new piece of music will have some clearly describable aspects; these will be listed at the start of each full transcription in the legend:

> **LEGEND**
>
> **Tuning:** a guitar tuning, standard or otherwise (most are in standard tuning).
>
> **Scale/Key:** a scale or key associated with the piece of music.
>
> **Picking:** a style of picking execution (with a plectrum, fingerstyle, or hybrid).
>
> **Sound:** a characteristic sound that (ideally) calls for a certain type of guitar or effect (acoustic steel-string, electric w/clean tone, etc.). As much as possible we'll stick to acoustic.

Each lesson provides some background on the instrument, its style and origins, a rundown of the techniques involved, and a full tune from its traditional repertoire. Scales and short technique demos are recorded wherever they're relevant. It's best to try playing along with the main track only after you've digested all this information.

Where there are backing tracks or multiple guitars, they are panned on separate sides of the mix so you can isolate the main part for closer study, or pan it out and play the main guitar part along with the backing tracks.

 ## Standard Tuning: (low to high) E–A–D–G–B–E

TRACK 01

THE LUTES

In the language of musicology, the word "lute" has come to refer to all plucked instruments with strings and fingerboards—not necessarily just the pear-shaped medieval/Renaissance instrument called *lute*, but everything you can sound by plucking and make note changes by placing fingers (or a slide) on its neck. The first such instrument in recorded history is said to have come from Asia Minor, and today they exist in endless varieties in every corner of the world. Most have frets, but there are many notable exceptions: the Japanese *shamisen*, the Indian *sarod*, and the Middle Eastern *oud*, to name a few. One of the oud's offspring, the modern *guitar*, is a relative newcomer that developed in Western Europe and has somehow become the most universal and popular lute. Luckily, it's versatile enough to play the music of many of its relatives.

Since the guitar is in familiar company, there are many lutes that can be covered. We'll travel geographically (and in no particular order of difficulty) from Latin America to Eastern Europe and the Middle East, through South and East Asia, and finally land in the South Pacific.

PUERTO RICAN
CUATRO

High-pitched lutes with double-string courses exist throughout the world. In the Americas and Europe, there seem to be common signature elements to their playing styles. They are often played in harmonizing pairs with certain staple techniques: arpeggios, tremolo picking, and lots of chromatic lines. This applies to the Greek *bouzouki*, the Spanish and Philippine *bandurria*, the Italian *mandolin*, the South American *charango*, and another product of Latin America by way of Iberia: the *cuatro*.

Different styles of cuatro exist throughout Latin America, but the Puerto Rican variety is perhaps the most popular. The offspring of various Portuguese and Spanish instruments, the cuatro originally had four courses of strings (hence the name; *cuatro* = four). The modern Puerto Rican cuatro has 10 strings in five courses—some in octaves, some unison—tuned from low to high: B–E–A–D–G. That makes it roughly compatible with standard guitar tuning; the challenge is to capture the high range and the shimmering effects of double-course strings.

The *seis* is a popular song style that grew from the rural *jibaro* music of Puerto Rico. "Seis Mapeyé" is a slow-tempo seis in which a singer improvises poetry over a string ensemble led by the cuatro. This tune traditionally has a pair of cuatros playing over a guitar and rhythm section; this arrangement will show you how to cover a double-cuatro melody with one guitar and use octaves and chromatic runs to solo in cuatro style.

Cuatro

Seis Mapeyé

TRACK 02

LEGEND

Tuning: standard

Key: D minor

Picking:
   guitar 1: dime & brush
   (see performance notes)

   guitars 2 and 3: plectrum

Sound:
   guitars 1 and 3 (cuatro): steel-string acoustic

   guitar 2 (guitar): nylon-string acoustic

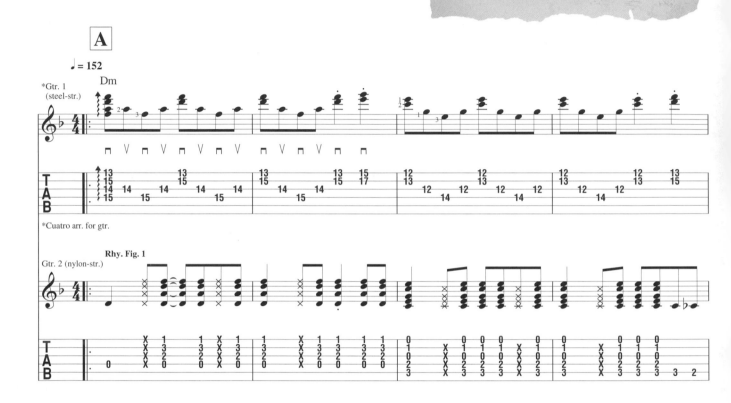

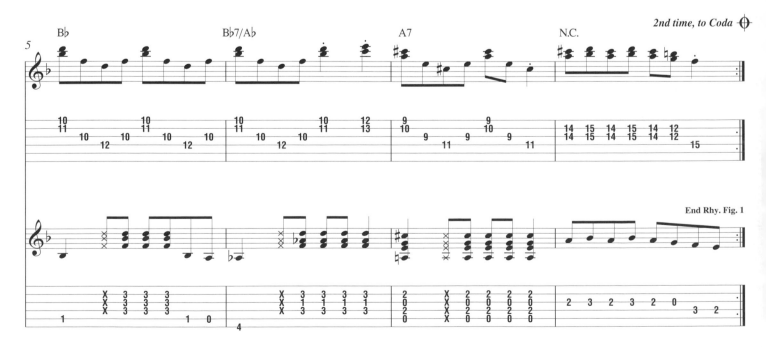

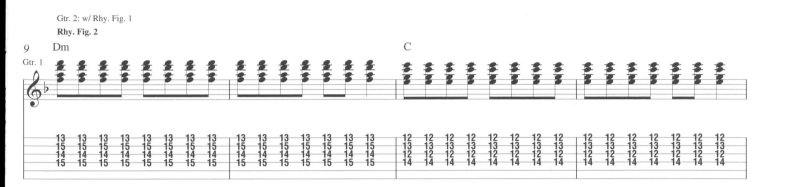

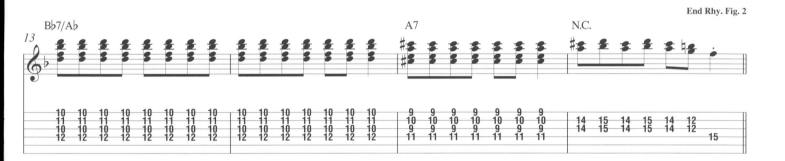

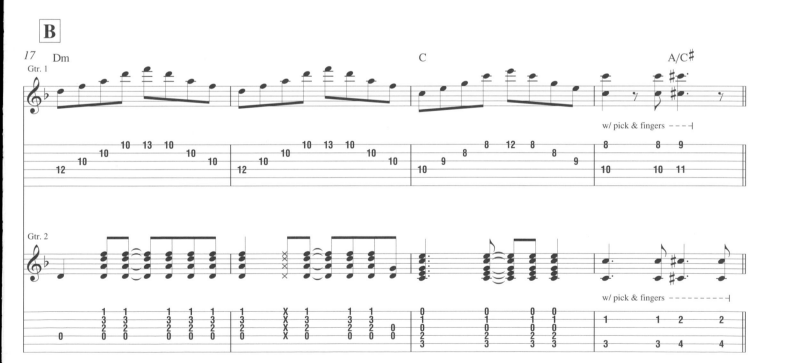

A

Gtr. 1: w/ Rhy. Fig. 2 (2 times, simile)
Gtr. 2: w/ Rhy. Fig. 1 (2 times)

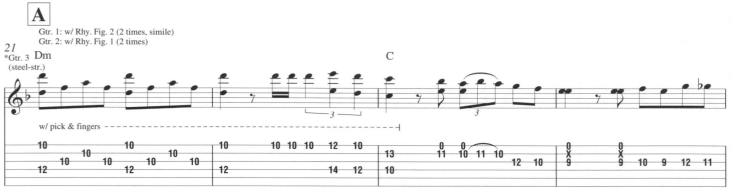

*Cuatro arr. for gtr.

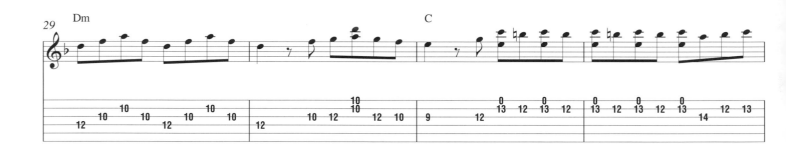

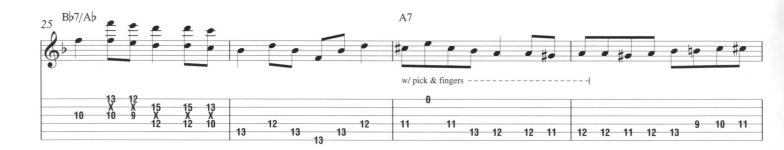

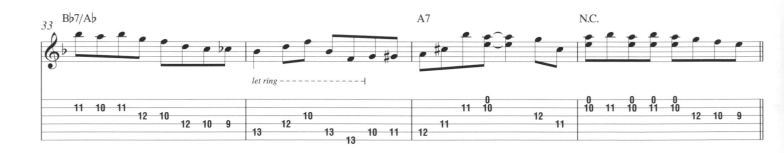

B

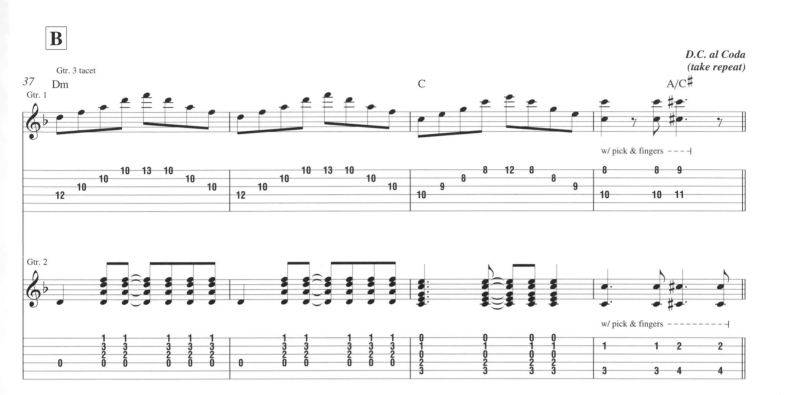

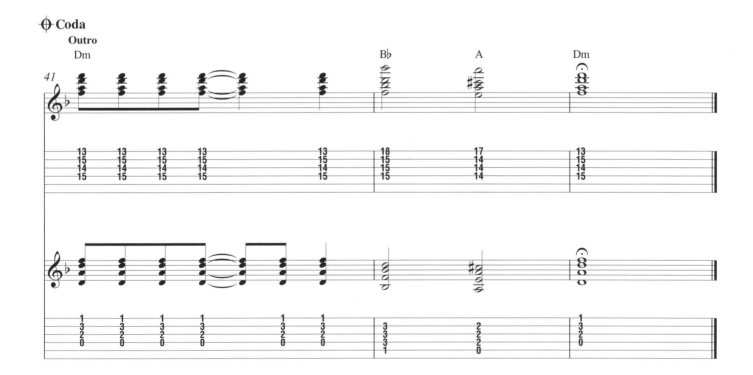

Seis Mapeyé Performance Notes

Picking the Proper Plectrum

To capture the bright-but-soft attack of the cuatro, try using a coin with a serrated edge as a pick. For Gtr. 1, a dime is the plectrum of choice in the A section. The solo (Gtr. 3) is played with a "real" pick for precision, but the cuatro part strummed underneath it (Gtr. 1) is played using a short-bristled brush (like a fingernail buffer) to get a soft attack with enhanced overtones.

Picking with a coin

Strumming with a brush

Cuatro Arpeggios

You see that the A section cuatro part is basically a series of *arpeggios* (chords played one note at a time) with a pair of notes played on top of each to suggest two instruments playing in harmony. There are suggested fingerings (numbers next to the notes) at the first and third measures of the A section; this shows how to hold a chord for each pair of measures and arpeggiate without too much tangling of the fingers. Also note the suggested picking pattern beneath the notation. You can play the harmony riff at the end of the A section with mini-*barres*, with one finger over each pair of strings.

Chromatic Octaves

The B section is a short interlude in which the singer would traditionally repeat a poetic phrase before beginning the next stanza or, in this case, hand it over to the cuatro for a solo. Here is another style of cuatro arpeggios, this time based on standard barre chords, followed by chromatically climbing octaves. Play the lower note with your pick and pluck the higher one with a free finger—this is one way to cover the sound of the cuatro's double courses on a single-course instrument.

The Cuatro Solo

The solo uses more arpeggios, octaves, and many chromatic runs to conjure up the cuatro's spirit. Notice the use of the open E string wherever it fits as a unison or harmony note; this is another way capture the color, if not the sound, of the cuatro's double courses.

RUSSIAN BALALAIKA

A Russian relative of the mandolin, the *balalaika* is a triangular-shaped, three-stringed instrument that comes in all sizes and ranges. Some balalaikas have six strings arranged in double courses (octaves or unisons) or four independently tuned strings. In a full balalaika orchestra, there is usually a huge bass balalaika (which often gets bolted to the floor for the sake of balance) and a couple of smaller, more common 'laikas in higher ranges, as well as a guitar and often a *domra*—a mandolin-like lute with a very high range. The orchestra's combined sound is huge and complex, like Russia itself.

Balalaika strings are traditionally gut or nylon, so a nylon-string guitar will get the closest sound. To accommodate the balalaika's high register, a capo is the best solution. The main guitar in the following example (Gtr. 1) is capoed at fret 5.

"The Moon Is Shining Brightly" is a popular Russian folk tune and a showcase of balalaika flashiness. Like many Russian folk songs, it starts out slowly and accelerates to breakneck speed. Here we'll keep it in one tempo for the sake of learning the tune.

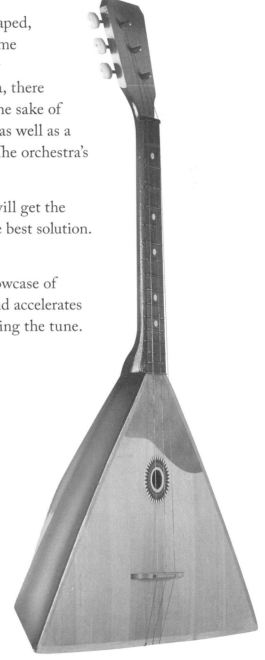

Balalaika

The Moon Is Shining Brightly

TRACK 03

Gtr. 1: Capo V

*Balalaika arr. for gtr.

**Symbols in parentheses represent chord names respective to capoed guitar. Symbols above reflect actual sounding chords. Capoed fret is "0" in tab.

The Moon Is Shining Brightly
Performance Notes

Strumming Brightly

The A section's balalaika part (Gtr. 1) is best played with quick alternate strumming from the wrist: "down–up–down–up–down, up, down–up–down–up–down, up, etc." (See the suggested strum pattern in meas. 1.) Barre the first fifth-fret chord with your index finger, so you can stretch out to frets 7 and 9 without a position shift.

Index finger barre on B and high E strings

The rhythm guitar (Gtr. 2) can be strummed with downstrokes, or (as on the recording) plucked with the thumb on the bass notes and fingers on the chords. Either way, you're best off picking your fret-hand fingers off the frets (but not off the strings) to dampen each chord immediately after you hit it; this will give the pattern a bright, energetic *staccato* feel, perfect for Russian folk dancing.

Chromatic Twirl

The B section might make you dizzy with its chromatic walking. Both parts (Gtr. 3 and Gtr. 4 [domra]) are good exercises for the fret-hand fingers; all your digits have to be involved! Use the "one-finger-per-fret" approach for both Gtr. 3 and 4—except on the position shift; the suggested fingerings to the left of the notes will show you where that happens.

Chop Chop

Meanwhile, the balalaika (Gtr. 1) chops dyads on the upbeats. Once again, make it staccato (to accommodate those squat-kicking dancers). You can do this with the left-hand damping technique described above or by resting the pick hand on the strings between "chops."

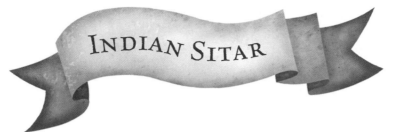

INDIAN SITAR

One of the guitar's South Asian cousins, the *sitar*, has long been a source of inspiration for musicians in the West. The Indian emphasis on improvisation makes it especially attractive to jazz musicians, while its stereotyped association with psychedelic pop grew mostly from the Beatles' George Harrison's association with Pandit Ravi Shankar in the sixties. What many Westerners don't know is that the *Hindustani* (North Indian classical) tradition from which the sitar comes is very strict and codified; within a system heavy on improvisation, every note you hear is played and accented according to a specific *raga*.

A raga is a kind of superscale—a modal, temporal, and spiritual outline for the music. There are thousands of different ragas, many with different ascending and descending forms. In most Indian music, the ornaments—slides, grace notes, and quarter-tone bends—are just as important as the notes themselves. It would take a few lifetimes to study all the intricacies of Indian music, so we'll graze the tip of the iceberg here with some sitar techniques.

The two primary styles of the sitar have six or seven plucked strings (three for drones and the rest for melody), beneath which are 11 or more *sympathetic strings* that resonate along with the main strings. Add that to a resonating bridge, and you have the constant "halo effect" of ringing overtones and drones. We can capture the essence of that effect on guitar by using drone strings and open tunings.

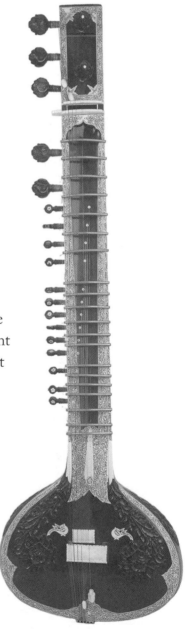

Get Horizontal

Lots of us have experienced the wonder of *horizontal scales* (going sideways across the neck on one string) and discovered how satisfying it can be to jam along with yourself by playing a horizontal melody over a ringing open string or two. You can get adept at this by scaling in *sequences* (repeated scale fragments) on the G string along with an open D-string drone. This requires lots of position shifting using just a few fingers (index, second, and third are recommended) and sliding them around like a sitarist, as shown in the Drone Exercise on the following page. Alternate pick as cleanly as you can, hitting both strings at once so the two sound as one—then slowly work it up to speed. You can do this on all adjacent string combinations. This example is in the very "Indianesque" D Lydian mode.

Sitar

Drone Exercise

*Key signature denotes D Lydian.

Indian Ornaments

In true South Asian traditions, rhythm and articulation are just as important as the notes themselves—there's no such thing as playing a "straight" melody, and everything is ornamented according to the raga. Here we're just trying to capture the flavor of a raga. Using the D string as a drone, take the most easily bendable intervals (half steps) of the D Lydian mode along the G string and use them for some strategic bends in a repeating, polyrhythmic phrase. Pull downward for your bends and vibrato.

Drone Riffs

TRACK 05

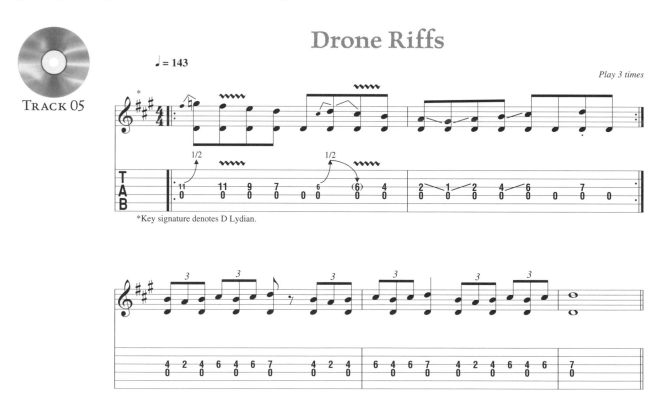

*Key signature denotes D Lydian.

Those last three measures comprise a kind of *tihai*, a thrice-repeating figure that Indian classical soloists play along with their percussionists as a climax for the end of a phrase. A tihai (from the Sanskrit word for "three") always ends on the first beat of the next beat cycle.

The best way to initiate yourself into Hindustani music is by learning "light classical" themes. Here is a *bhajan* (religious song) that was one of Mahatma Ghandi's favorites, played with the traditional backing of a *tanpura* (drone instrument) and *tabla* drums.

Bhajan: Vaishnava Janato

TRACK 07

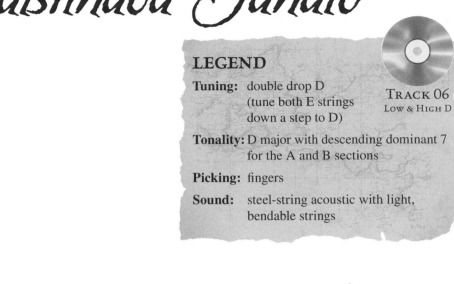

LEGEND

Tuning: double drop D
(tune both E strings
down a step to D)

TRACK 06
LOW & HIGH D

Tonality: D major with descending dominant 7
for the A and B sections

Picking: fingers

Sound: steel-string acoustic with light,
bendable strings

Double Drop D tuning:
(low to high) D–A–D–G–B–D

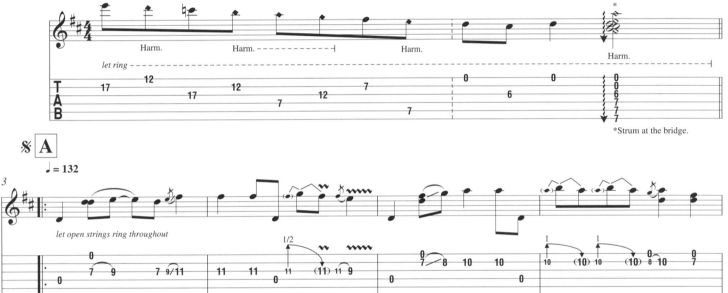

D.S. al Coda 1
(no repeat)

⊕ Coda 1

C

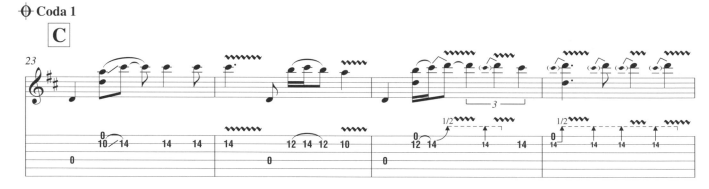

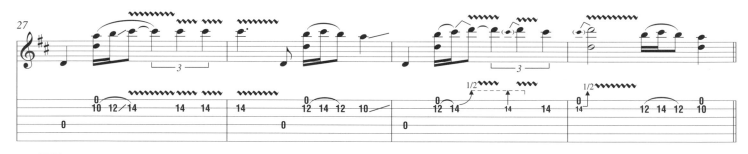

B

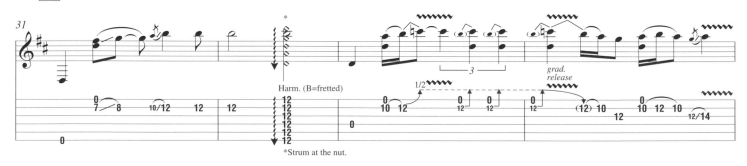

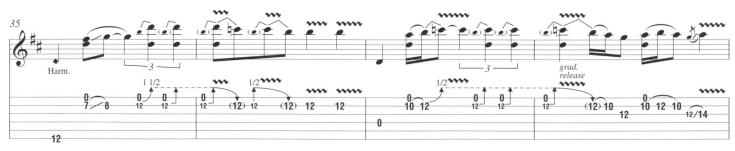

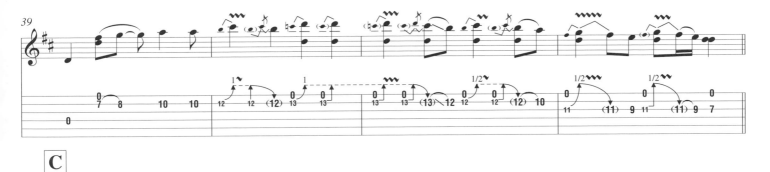

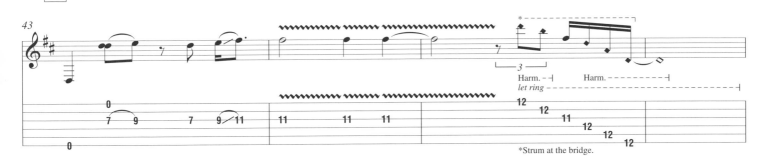

*Strum at the bridge.

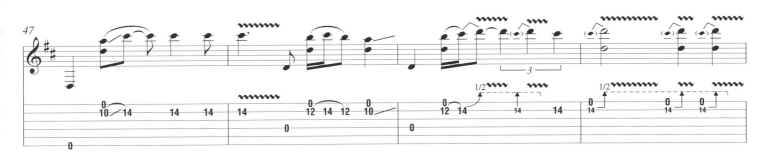

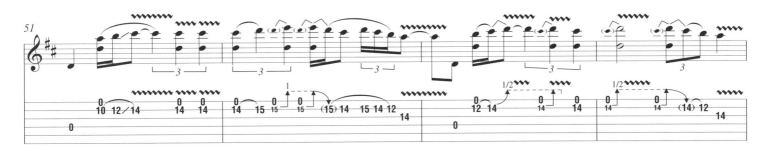

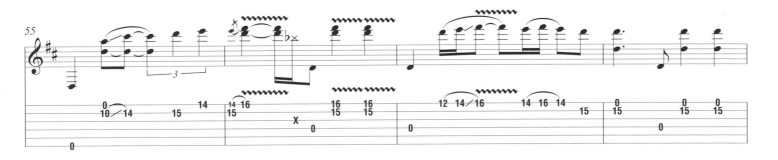

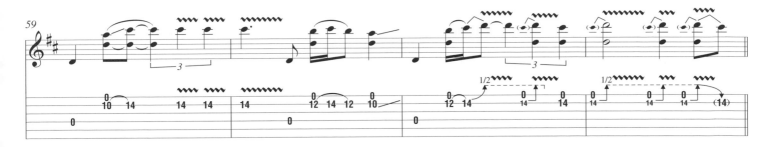

*Strum at the nut.

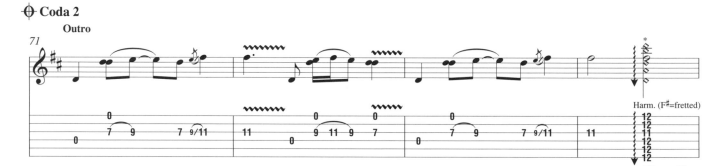

D.S. al Coda 2
(no repeat)

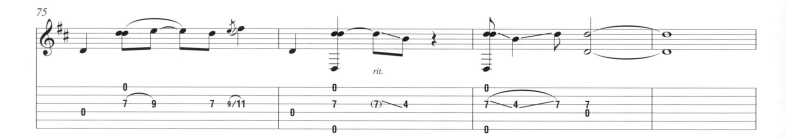

*Strum at the bridge.

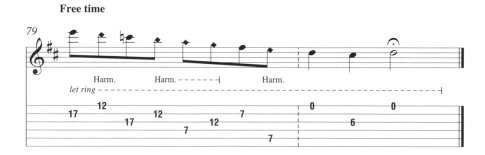

Bhajan: Vaishnava Janato

Performance Notes

This bhajan has an interesting layout. It establishes an A–B structure (totaling 28 measures), and on repeats of that structure, a variable C section gets inserted into the A and B sections without changing their total combined length. This is one example of Indian music's flexibility within a strict framework.

Sympathetic Shimmer

The opening flourish simulates the effect of the sitar's sympathetic drone strings when the player plucks them to create shimmering glissando effects. The guitar doesn't shimmer in quite the same way, but the combination of fretted and harmonic notes gives the same effect of close intervals. Notice the position of the downward-arpeggiated chord: seventh-fret harmonics mixed with open and fretted strings. Run your picking finger down the strings from the bridge.

Combination of fretted, open, and harmonic notes

In double drop D tuning, you have three open D notes to help recreate the "halo effect" of the sitar's sympathetic and plucked drone strings. The open middle-D string provides a foundation, while the upper drone string creates tension and release when mixed with bends of the B and G strings below. Bending, by the way, is how sitarists create *meends*—smooth note movement in quarter tones—a signature sound in Indian music.

Hindustani Blues

One characteristic of sitar playing is a fast-but-subtle vibrato that often comes along with a wider string bend or at the end of a quick hammer-on/pull-off (meas. 4). Blues players know that vibrato on a bent note helps you stay in pitch; it also gives the "singing" quality that most Hindustani instrumentalists seek to emulate.

Mood Swings

Pre-bends are also prominent in the sitar world, and those who don't bend to an accurate pitch are doomed to remain apprentices forever. Notice that at the point where a pre-bend is released into a downward slide (meas. 9), the tonality has changed! What was a major 7 (C♯) on the way up is now a *dominant* 7 (C♮). The sudden, emotive appearance of the ♭7 is something you'll hear in a lot of ragas as well as Indian folk songs. It is also a universal "blue note" common in jazz and country music in the West.

The B and C sections introduce another neo-sitar technique: *hammering into a bend* (meas. 13). This captures the sound of a quick multi-step bend from one position on the sitar. Watch out for the following *step-and-a-half bend*, which needs to be accurate and drop smoothly from 1½ steps (bent) to ½ step (bent) and release, with a dash of vibrato. If some of these bends seem hard on the fingers, imagine the work of the sitarist who (in addition to extreme bending) wears a tight metal wire around the picking finger and sits cross-legged, holding up a large instrument for hours at a time!

Backwards Ornaments

In the C section, you'll find a return of the major 7 and more hammers into bends, followed by a B section variation with another downward arpeggio in the style of sympathetic-string ornaments.

This time, the 12th-fret harmonics are strummed along with a fretted B note, from the *opposite side*, by running your picking finger down the strings *at the nut* (on the fretboard side). Why, you ask? Two main reasons: (1) the fretted B note is allowed to sustain undisturbed, while (2) plucked from the other side, the same string at the same fret sounds as a C♯—creating a dissonance that previews the return of the ♭7 (a normally-fretted C♮) in the following measure.

Strumming at the nut

Strumming at the bridge

The tune continues through many rhythmic and melodic variations of these three sections, illustrating the relative freedom Indian musicians have to express themselves within a strict structure. More drone-string ornaments appear, including one at the outro with a fretted F♯ under 12th-fret harmonics (strummed at the bridge). The outro is a kind of tihai, repeating the melody three times, ending with a three-beat rhythmic device, and crowning it all with the same drone-string flourish that opened the tune.

More tunes and techniques from the Hindustani and *Carnatic* (South Indian classical) traditions are covered in the book/CD *World Guitar*.

CHINESE PIPA

The ravishing Chinese counterpart to the guitar, the *pipa*, is a pear-shaped, four-stringed lute instrument with a thin body and scalloped frets, conducive to pre-bends, delicate picking, and fast, undulating vibrato—enticing and intimidating to the humble guitarist. The pipa player plays the whole instrument, creating percussion and other sound effects, pulling the strings in wide bends, and fanning the strings with the backs of the fingers for smooth tremolo picking. We won't do all of that here, but we will explore some novel techniques that capture the spirit of the pipa.

"Yizu Wuqu" ("Dance of the Yi People") is a popular pipa version of a Sichuan folk tune. An excerpt from its first movement was covered as one of the lessons in the book/CD *World Guitar*. Here is what can be considered the second of three movements; it begins where the *World Guitar* excerpt left off and introduces some new pipa-style techniques.

This tune is typically played with rhythmic as well as articulate dynamics; it speeds up and slows down as it builds and lowers intensity, somewhat like the fugue or sonata of Western classical music. For learning purposes, it follows a straight tempo here, but you are encouraged to check out some authentic pipa versions of this tune (you can find it on almost any recording of pipa music) and experience the true dynamics of the piece.

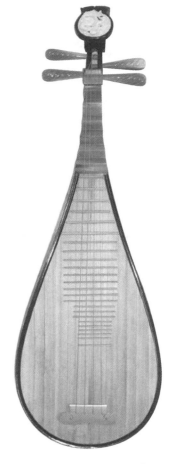

Pipa

Yizu Wuqu
(Dance of the Yi People), 2nd Movement

LEGEND

Tuning: standard

Key: A minor

Picking: A section: plectrum

B section: fingers

Sound: acoustic steel-string

TRACK 08

A

Brightly, with feeling ♩ = 116

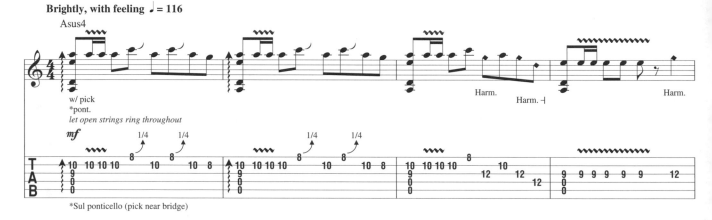

w/ pick
*pont.
let open strings ring throughout

*Sul ponticello (pick near bridge)

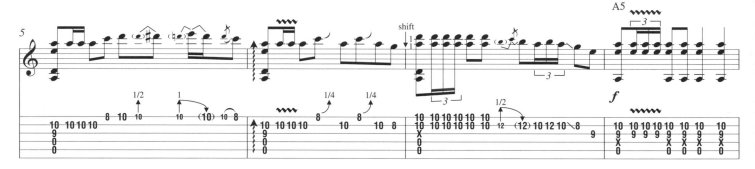

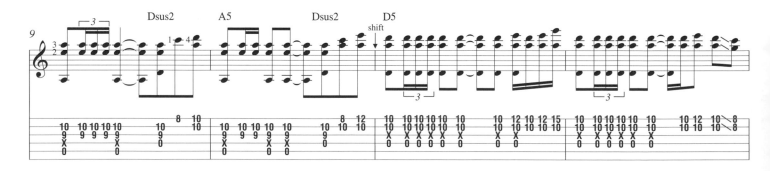

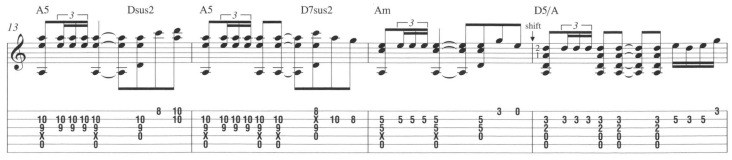

Yizu Wuqu Performance Notes

The pipa's standard tuning is A–D–E–A. That makes standard guitar tuning somewhat pipa-friendly, and the ringing of the open A and D strings under a chord is typical in pipa music—turning what could have been an A5 chord into a very Chinese Asus4.

Asian Acrobatics

Begin with a pick and strum close to the bridge (*sul ponticello*) for a bright tone. As much as possible, add a dash of expressive vibrato to each group of triplets. This kind of ornament, an upward-bending vibrato on a sustained or repeated note, is emblematic in Chinese music of all kinds, especially on the pipa. Pull downward for your vibrato, but play the following quarter-step bends with a push upward. (These reside in what blues aficionados refer to as the "B.B. King box.") At some points, harmonics are combined with fretted notes; this is not just to make your life difficult, but to get a sound that is as authentically "Asian" as possible.

However organic this piece may sound, it is totally pre-composed, so it helps to be a step ahead of yourself on the fretboard. Position shifts are noted above the staff, and there are suggested fingerings to the left of the notes wherever they might be helpful. Also note the Xs in the tab where strings are muted.

Chinese Finger Puzzles

At the B section, the pick drops (quickly!) and the bizarreness commences. This is where the pipa player would "fan" the strings with the backs of the fingernails for the upper tremolo-picked notes while plucking the bass line with the thumb. Such a technique, as played on the vertically-oriented pipa (with the neck pointing to the sky), is not easily done on the horizontal guitar. Nor is classical guitar-style tremolo picking the best way to go, as it tends to leave a pause in the tremolo-picked notes every time the thumb plucks.

Here is an alternative solution: a fast, constant flutter of the middle finger while the thumb plucks the bass notes. With some practice, this will give you a smooth tremolo with all the subtleties of the pipa style, especially when combined with more expressive vibrato.

Also notice that the low-E string, so far neglected, comes in handy as a 12th-fret harmonic when the "fluttering" happens at the upper frets.

Pipa-style tremolo

JAPANESE SHAMISEN

The *shamisen* is a fretless three-stringed lute with a long, thin neck and a stretched-skin head on the body which resonates somewhat like a banjo. It is picked with a large, weighted plectrum called a *bachi*. The shamisen is played very percussively, often with a technique that has the bachi striking the string and the head at the same time. The bridge is designed to make the strings buzz, somewhat like an Indian *sitar*. Distinctive slides and pronounced vibrato are hallmarks of most shamisen styles, which vary in Japan according to region and tradition.

The Pick that Goes "Ping"

Just for now, ignore the sage advice of guitar teachers who might have told you to avoid string noise and to pick conservatively. Feel free to smack the strings with your pick; it's the best way to get the percussive attack of the shamisen. Play close to the bridge; that will keep your strings from going out of pitch and add more of that desirable "ping." Experiment with different picking implements: a copper pick will give you extra bite and a coin with serrated edges (like a dime or a Euro ten-cent coin) will roughen the attack. For the following examples, a triangular Tortex pick was used for precision and sharpness.

Shamisen

Playing in the Box

The following tune, and the scale that comprises it, can be approached in a neo-blues fashion, leaving the D string open for the drone while shifting between pentatonic "boxes" that fall in two general areas of the neck:

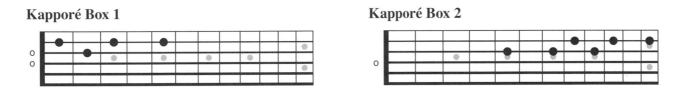

Kapporé Box 1   **Kapporé Box 2**

These boxes outline a minor pentatonic scale with the tones: 1–2–4–5–♭7. Or literally: 1, 4, 5, ♭7, 8 (1), 9 (2). This is an extension of the *yo* scale, one of many traditional Japanese modes, with the ♭7 added:

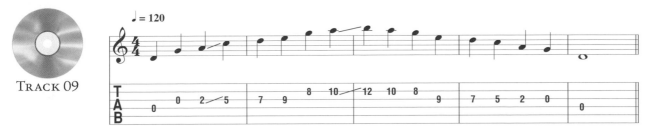

"Kapporé" is a popular Japanese dance tune with a comical feel. The shamisen melody outlines the vocal that is traditionally sung over it while providing a rhythmic foundation for the song. (In a tune like this, drums are used more as punctuation than timekeepers—now that's your job!)

Kappoŕé

TRACK 10

LEGEND

Tuning: standard

Tonality: "Yo" scale extension in D

Picking: hard pick with a sharp edge

Sound: small-bodied nylon-string guitar

A

Moderately ♩ = 105

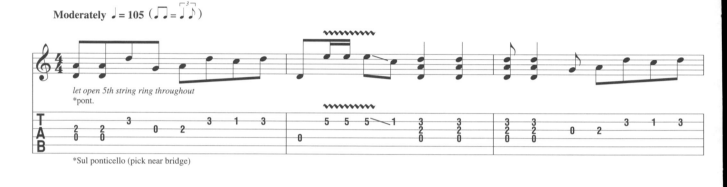

let open 5th string ring throughout
*pont.

*Sul ponticello (pick near bridge)

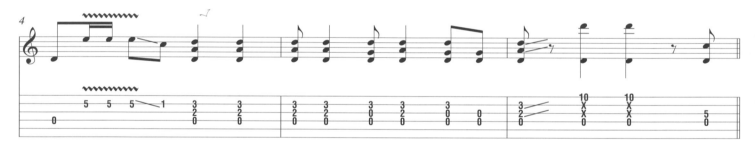

B

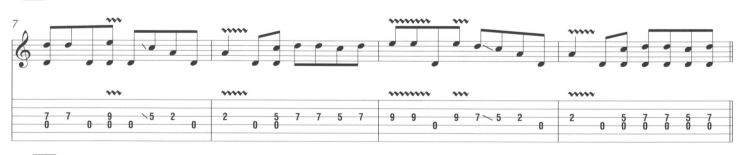

C

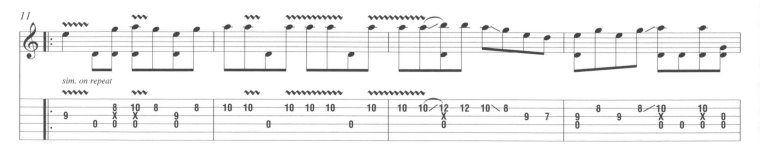

sim. on repeat

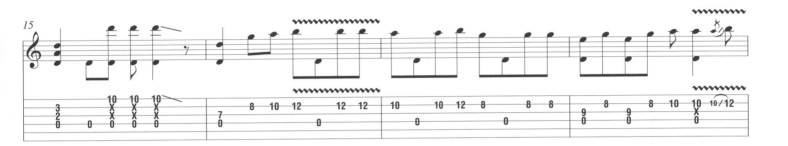

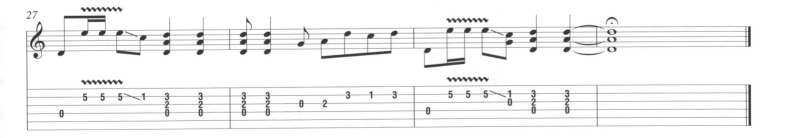

 *Kapporé* Performance Notes

Japanese Shuffle

This arrangement of "Kapporé" maps itself in three basic sections of varying lengths, punctuated by short breaks where chants are traditionally shouted when the intro phrase returns or a high D is repeated. Your first important task as timekeeper is to keep the distinctive, moderate shuffle that is emblematic of much traditional Japanese and Korean music while keeping the melody flowing.

Conventional guitar wisdom says that a shuffle is played "down–up, down–up, etc.," with the downstroke as a long beat and the upstroke a short one. Throw that out the window for now, and think of this generally as a "down–down" blues shuffle with exceptions: sometimes, as on the 3rd-fret D note, an upstroke works for the long beat and the sixteenth notes are always alternate picked. Imagine that you're attacking the strings with a heavy bachi, so your shuffling is more like that of a drummer than a guitarist.

Twang!

On the fretless shamisen, vibrato is made horizontally with a sideways "shake" of the fretting hand. The result is an elastic sound that markedly raises the note's pitch with each vibration. East Asian music in general uses this kind of expressive ornament; you'll often hear it in the music of the Chinese *erhu* (spike fiddle) and the Korean *kayagum* (zither), but it is especially pronounced on the shamisen. The guitarist can get the same effect with bending vibrato, pulling the affected string downward in order to stay out of the way of the droning D string. Give the B string a good shake every time you play the 5th-fret sixteenth notes in the A section. If you're playing a nylon-string (recommended), you'll know that it requires a little more pulling than a steel-string to get the right amount of "twang." Use extra fingers behind the fretting finger to give it more strength.

Vibrato with extra fingers behind fretting finger

Keep the open-D string droning between melody notes, and notice that when a B- or E-string note is played along with the open D, the intervening strings are *dampened* to keep them from ringing out (as shown with Xs in tab). This keeps you true to the melodically spacious sound of Japanese music, and the extra dampened strings add to the percussive attack characteristic of the shamisen.

THAI PHIN

The *phin* (pronounced "pin") is a lute from Northeastern Thailand which usually has two or three metal strings and a diatonic fretboard. Originally derived from the South Indian *veena*, it is far removed from its parent instrument, looking more like a mandolin/dulcimer hybrid with a decorated dragon headstock. It was traditionally used for vocal accompaniment, especially in courtship. Some modern phins are electrified and often played with distortion and other effects (as used in the *Isaan* folk music of Northeastern Thailand and Laos). Depending on the tuning, the frets can play hexatonic scales that are close to Dorian or Mixolydian modes, although in traditional tunings, some notes are tempered differently from Western standards. The music has slight Chinese, Indian, and Indonesian flavors, but a uniquely Thai groove and structure.

Shredding over a Drone

In typical phin music, one string is used as a repeating drone while the player shifts around the upper "melody" string, interspersing fast pull-offs and bouncing between open and fretted positions. The phin's open strings are often tuned in 5ths, but 4ths are prominent in the tunes. Therefore, the B and high-E strings (the tonic and the 4th, respectively) are close enough in interval and range to approximate the phin sound.

Phin

Phin Solo

LEGEND

Tuning: standard

Tonality: B Dorian

Sound: steel-string acoustic

Picking: pick close to the bridge for a trebly tone

TRACK 11

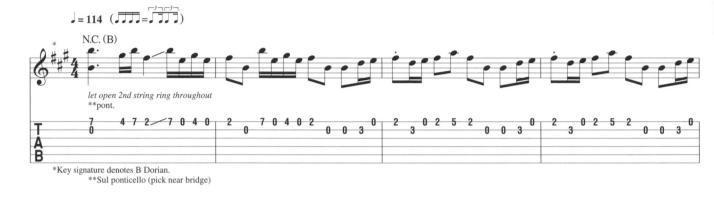

let open 2nd string ring throughout
**pont.

*Key signature denotes B Dorian.
**Sul ponticello (pick near bridge)

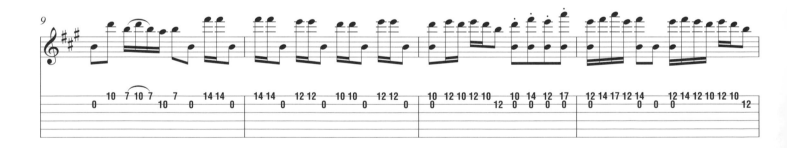

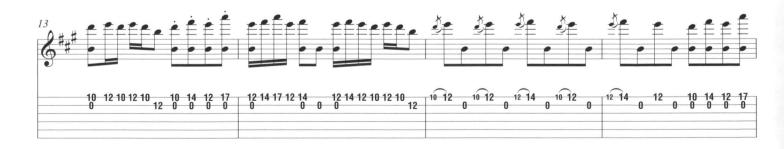

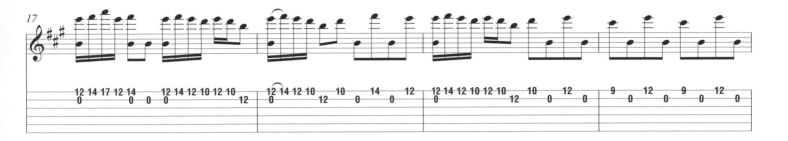

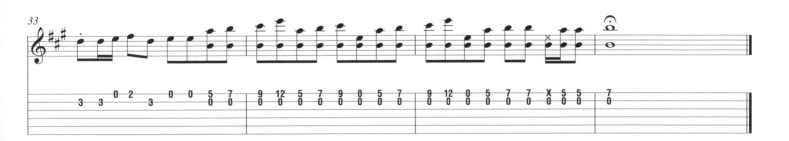

Phin Solo Performance Notes

This sixteenth-note shuffle tune pulses like a palpitating heartbeat after a bite of hot green curry but manages to keep the carefree peacefulness of Thai music. It is built on repeated and varied phrases, using subtle changes in tonality to build interest.

Sawatdee Shuffle

You are now free to recall the conventional guitar wisdom that says a fast shuffle is best played "down–up, down–up," with a downstroke for the long beat and an upstroke for the short beat. Imagine your hand moving in constant sixteenth notes while you pick selectively and "miss" the strings when not playing sixteenths. Don't literally keep your hand bouncing all the time, but keep the groove in your mind. The down- and upstrokes are not strict either, just a general guideline for this kind of fast Asian swing.

Alternate picking is also important for bouncing between open and fretted notes on the E string. Notice that these moves are not done as hammer-ons and pull-offs but picked cleanly every time. You will get the chance to hammer and pull in other spots, notably the grace notes in measures 15 and 16.

Change of Mood

Notice the sudden appearance of a C♯ note (E string, fret 9) in measure 20— adding a 2nd to the relatively small number of notes in this tune and dramatically changing the direction of the piece. This is just one example of how a change in tonality over a drone, rather than a key change in a chord progression, can make a great impact.

Staccato Stings

You might have noticed the great number of *staccato* (dotted) notes in this piece. These are best nailed by taking your fret-hand finger off the fretboard—but not off the string—immediately after you pick the note, creating a percussive "sting" for extra energy.

Remember our favorite word, *sul ponticello*: pick close to the bridge for a tone with extra sting. This will also help you keep pitch control while you're strumming heavily.

The guitar's diminutive cousin, the *ukulele* is an instrument that developed in Hawaii from a Portuguese prototype. Though ukuleles come in various sizes and configurations, the most common is the *soprano*, which usually has four nylon strings (originally gut) tuned G–C–E–A (top to bottom) and a mini-guitar body.

Aloha Shuffle

The "aloha" sound of Hawaiian music is rife with *major 6th* and dominant 7th chords and, more often than not, swings! This usually means that in a strum pattern, your downstrokes will last longer than your upstrokes, so you get the heartbeat-style groove of an eighth-note shuffle. (See the swing indicator at the start of the music below.) The following exercise will be good for shuffling practice.

One quick-and-easy way to cover the ukulele sound on a standard guitar is with *palm muting*, resting the pick hand on the strings over the guitar's bridge while you strum. This will give each strum a short decay, mimicking the choppy sound of the small-bodied uke. The chords you fret should be in small, three- or four-note clusters. Here is a short example of how a British Invasion pop group might have played a uke-style pattern on guitar: with palm muting, triads, swing feel, and the requisite major 6th chord.

Ukulele

Uke Strumming

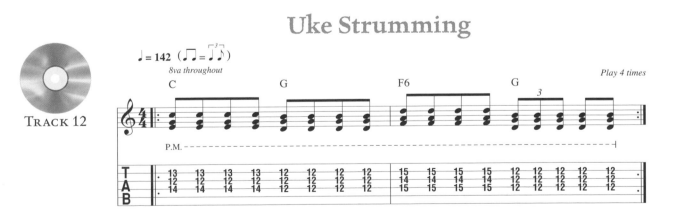

TRACK 12

That's one approach; here is another that allows you to strum chords while playing a melody. Stay in standard guitar tuning, but use a capo to bring it up to the soprano uke's range. Using nylon strings and familiar chord fingerings, you can cover the archetypal Hawaiian song on your pseudo-ukulele.

Aloha Oe

LEGEND

Tuning: standard

Key: C major (on an eighth-fret capoed guitar, the actual key is A♭)

Picking: fingerpick the opening verse; strum the choruses with index finger

Sound: nylon-string guitar (capo VIII)

TRACK 13

Capo VIII

Moderately ♩ = 143

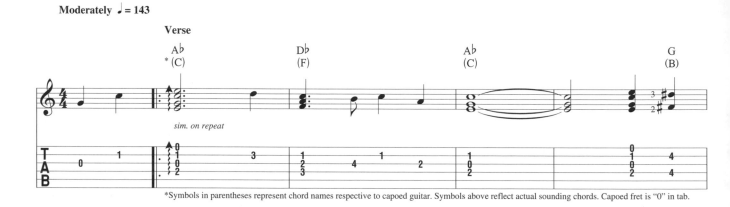

*Symbols in parentheses represent chord names respective to capoed guitar. Symbols above reflect actual sounding chords. Capoed fret is "0" in tab.

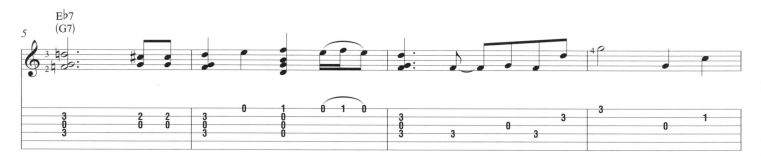

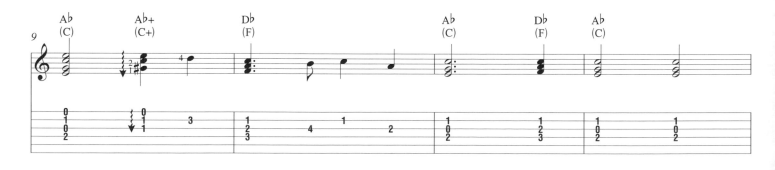

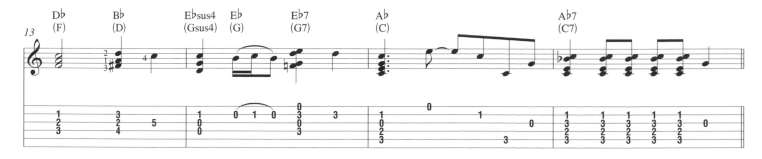

Chorus

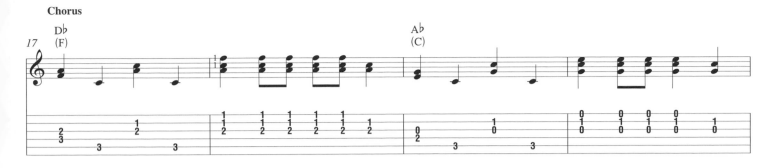

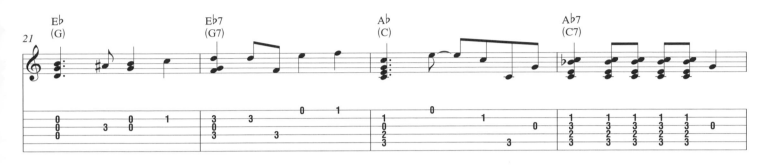

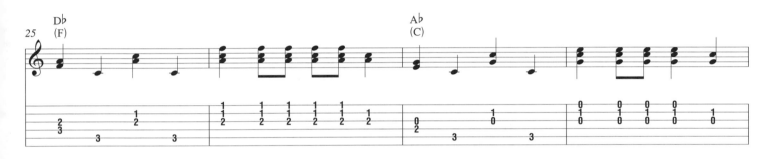

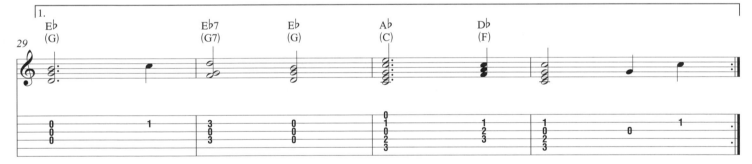

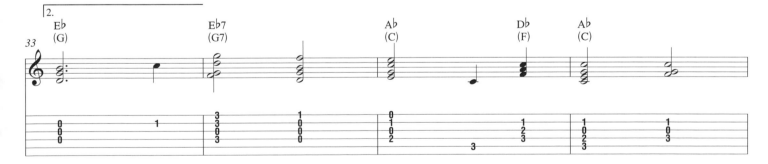

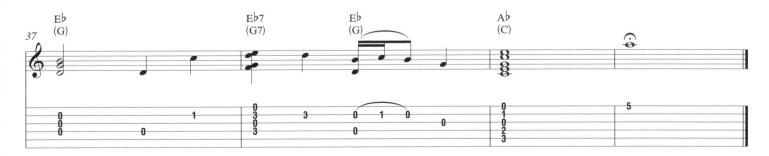

Aloha Oe Performance Notes

The most conventional Western-style tune in this volume, "Aloha Oe" has a melody built largely on *arpeggios*, making it easy to play on the pseudo-uke while strumming your own accompaniment. Since an arpeggio is basically a chord played one note at a time, you can hold each chord while picking the melody. The best course of action is to walk through the progression, get familiar with the chords, then work in the melody notes. This is best played fingerstyle, with some plucking for the verses and strumming with the index finger for the choruses.

Suggested fingerings are placed to the left of the notes wherever they might not be second nature. Chord shapes and movement are as true to ukulele style as possible, including the passing G (B) and A♭+ (C+) in the verse, the slightly dissonant E♭7 (G7) voicing, and chromatic passing notes when they fit with the melody. The final A♭ (C) turns into a 6th chord with the addition of a 5th-fret A note for the final measure. Nothing says "aloha" like a major 6th!

Pinky finger playing the major 6th

Finally, keep the shuffle in mind, even though it doesn't start swinging until the chorus that introduces eighth notes. The old guitar-shuffle strumming axiom applies here: a downstroke is a long beat; an upstroke is a short beat.

HARPS AND ZITHERS

Just like the lute, most cultures seem to have harp traditions. An instrument classified as a *harp* may have been one of the first stringed instruments, consisting of a plucked string stretched between two points (i.e., a bow). Of course, most harps have a full range of strings, and each string is usually a fixed pitch (except when bent, as on the *koto*). We can consider a *zither* as any kind of harp with a soundboard or resonating box beneath it. This includes the plucked and "hammered" varieties.

The key characteristic of the harp and zither sound is the way their notes ring into each other, creating dissonances and haunting textures. As you'll see, that calls for some very exotic approaches on guitar.

WEST AFRICAN KORA

The *kora* looks something like a cross between a sitar and a harp, with a large resonating gourd body, a neck-like column, and at least 21 strings (arranged in two sets) that radiate from it. One of many traditional instruments that is unique to the African sub-Sahara, the kora is played in complex, polyphonic grooves spiced with ostinato riffs. The player anchors each hand on a post while plucking with the thumb and index finger. Some of the great African guitarists have been influenced by the kora tradition and the results are mesmerizing.

Kora players have a distinctive style of glissando playing that selectively clusters and crushes notes together in tight intervals, similar (but not that similar) to what some jazz pianists do. Three interesting ways to deal with this are outlined here and revisited in the full tune that follows.

Kora

Trickle Down

Use a technique familiar to most guitarists: the *pull-off*. Here is an example that falls down the E Dorian mode a couple octaves from the high G to middle B, using sequenced, three-note pull-offs (and slides) on the high E and B strings. Let the open low-E string ring out for reference as you trickle down the neck.

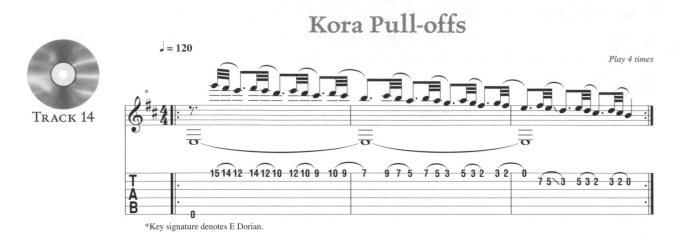

*Key signature denotes E Dorian.

Down Is Up

To really nail the kora sound, we have to let some strings ring out whilst "glissandizing." (Is that a word? We'll make it one.) Here's a technique that mixes fretted and open strings that fit conveniently in an E minor tonality. It also warps your guitar reality a little bit. Note the picking pattern: index (i), middle (m), thumb (p), etc.

Half Raked

Technique number three gets even closer to real kora playing with *rakes* across two strings combined with plucked open notes. Note the fingering again: for each group of three notes, the index finger sweeps upward across two fretted strings, and the middle finger plucks an open string.

Kora Rakes

TRACK 16

All three techniques are put to use in the following tune: a swinging, slightly hypnotic, Gambian-style kora vamp that is traditionally sung or chanted over.

43

Kora Song

TRACK 17

LEGEND

Tuning: standard

Tonality: E Dorian

Picking: fingerstyle

Sound: steel-string acoustic

Intro
Moderate shuffle ♩ = 144

Play 4 times

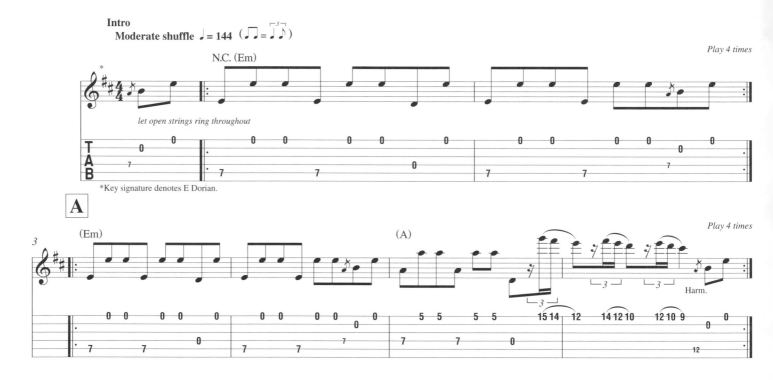

let open strings ring throughout

Key signature denotes E Dorian.

A

Play 4 times

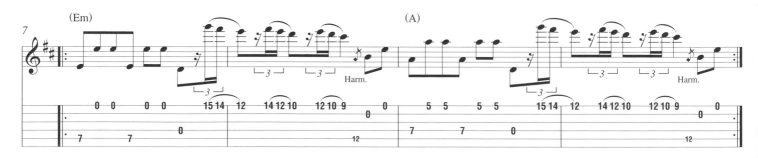

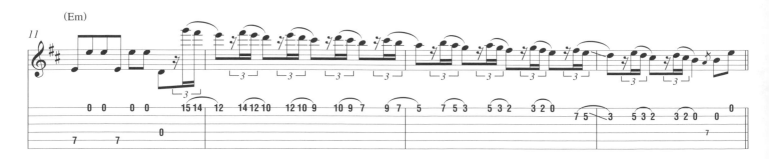

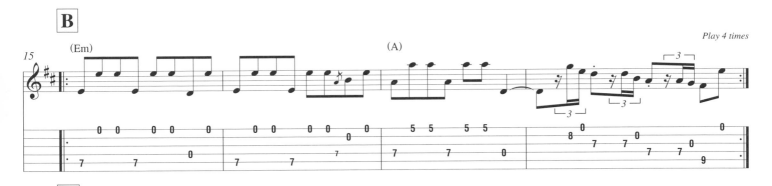

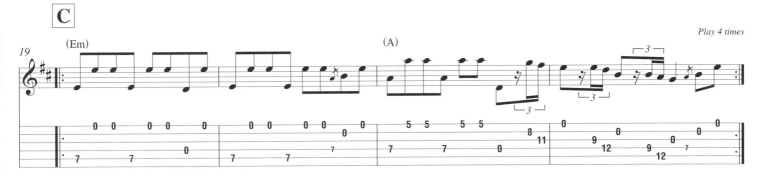

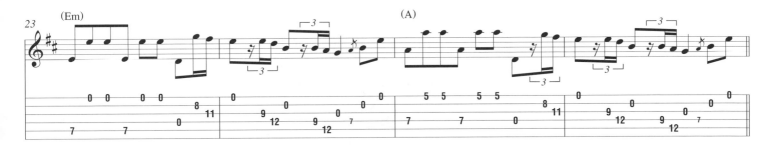

Kora Song Performance Notes

Swing It!

In this relaxed shuffle pattern, each pair of eighth notes gets a long and short beat, but don't sweat the technical jargon; just consider it more like a heartbeat than your standard "straight-eighths" pattern. As you can see throughout this book, the natural tendency is to shuffle more often than not, and somewhere in the course of human history we have become too regimented to remember that.

Fling It!

The opening measures give you some practice on another essential kora lick: an upward "fling" across two adjacent notes that ring into each other, creating an effect similar to what drummers call a *flam*. To begin, pluck the A grace note (fret 7 on the D string) with your thumb, and follow it immediately with your index finger on the open-B string. Generally, throughout this piece you can use your thumb on the lower notes and alternate between index and middle fingers on the upper notes.

The Path of Least Resistance

Notice that after the pull-off riff (meas. 6), the A grace note is a 12th-fret harmonic; that's because you just played a riff that ends with your first finger on fret 9 of the high-E string. Rather than cutting that note short to make a quick shift down the neck, you can reach your ring (or pinky) finger over to the A-string, 12th-fret harmonic to proceed smoothly.

Playing harmonic with ring finger

After you've broken in the first set of riffs, they become more frequent, and the extended pull-off riff acts as a transition between different variations of the main pattern. The B section is a rhythmic as well as melodic variation. The "half-raked" C section repeats and doubles up, and a series of triplets outlines the E minor pentatonic scale to close.

An array of harmonic and fretted techniques can be used to conjure up the spirit of the *koto*, a large zither with a sound and playing style that are distinctly Japanese. The koto sound is somewhat unique among harp instruments, partly because of the playing techniques used: the strings are often bent behind their moveable bridges to change their pitch; there are distinctive glissando styles and pick-scrape sound effects as well.

Koto

An effective way to translate koto and other harp-style sounds to the guitar is by using harmonics combined with fretted notes to make each note ring into the next as much as possible. This means that you're often skipping around the fretboard to find different fingerings for the same note depending on where the preceding or following harmonic falls in relation to it. Even though you're not in an alternate tuning, the landscape of the neck becomes very different.

Harmonic Lick #1

Here's a combination of harmonics that outlines the E minor pentatonic scale with an added 9th, just by bouncing between the 7th and 12th fret on strategic strings. Lines like this are nice as textural fills or exotic additions to solos. This will help prepare your hand for the arrangement of "Sakura" to come.

Koto Harmonics #1

TRACK 18

Harmonic Lick #2

Now try it up an octave, on the 3rd and 5th frets. This is a good way to develop your accuracy in the realm of upper-stratosophere harmonics.

Koto Harmonics #2

TRACK 19

In Scale

The mystique of the koto comes not only from its sound but also from the tonalities of its music. A lot of koto music draws from the *In* scale, a five-note grouping that is big in traditional Japanese court music. Here is the scale played straight (in A):

In Scale

TRACK 20

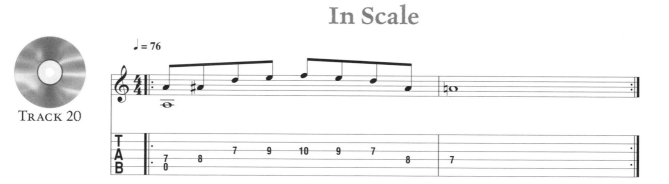

Neo-Koto Licks

Here are some koto-style flourishes from the In scale. Precise bends, tremolo picking, and glissandos like these are koto staples. (If your G string is too heavy for this bend, use a quick two-fret slide-and-return.) Note the suggested fret-hand fingerings on harmonics and fretted notes.

Koto Licks

TRACK 21

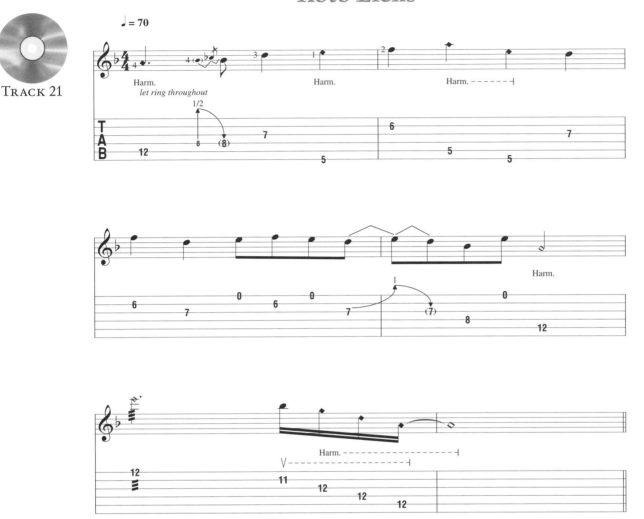

Kumoi-Joshi Scale

The previous techniques can be combined with fretted notes to play a traditional Japanese tune, koto-style. "Sakura" is an emblematic song for the annual Spring Cherry Blossom Festival. Many koto arrangements of this tune exist, in which the basic melody is stated and then played in different variations. But first, here is the scale for "Sakura." It's another pentatonic scale called *kumoi-joshi*, and it sounds like this:

Kumoi-Joshi Scale

TRACK 22

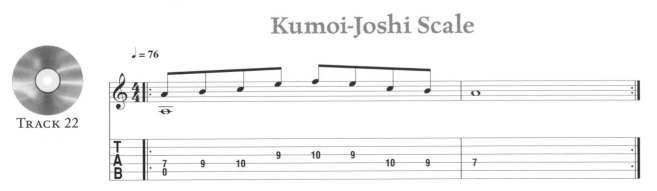

Now here is "Sakura" played koto style in three verses: first the straight melody, then two variations.

Sakura

TRACK 23

LEGEND

Tuning: standard

Tonality: Kumoi-Joshi scale in A

Picking: fingerstyle

Sound: steel-string acoustic

Sakura Performance Notes

If you've heard this tune played on koto, you might notice that this version is transposed up a step from the standard koto tuning. This is to accommodate the guitar's harmonic landscape. If you want to play it in the typical key of G, tune your guitar down a step.

The Basics

The first verse states the basic melody with a combination of harmonics and fretted notes. At the end of the first statement (meas. 4), E and F notes are played together—no, it's not a mistake, but a kind of deliberate dissonance that is distinctly Japanese and characteristic of koto playing. Tension and release are created, not by Western-style chord changes, but by tight intervals like this. Notice that on some of the fretted notes, subtle vibrato is created with a quick pull-and-release of the string (meas. 5–6, etc.).

Main fretboard shape

Verse 2

See the suggested fingerings where they're shown in the notation and get comfortable in this position: with your fret-hand index finger riding around the 7th fret, your pinky at fret 12, and your ring finger often fretting at the 10th fret. You'll be here for a while…

Now that you know the basics, here comes the fun part. The melody stays the same but is surrounded by neo-counterpoint embellishments in the same fretted/harmonic style. Again, fingerings are written where they might be helpful. The second verse ends with another koto-style flourish: a downward arpeggio combining open, fretted, and harmonic notes.

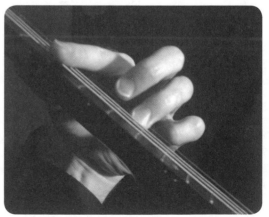

Fingering for downward arpeggio

Verse 3

The third verse introduces octaves (another common koto technique) played with harmonics and more embellishments around the melody, including repeated open E notes. Play these classical guitar-style, alternating between the 2nd and 1st plucking fingers, respectively—or if you are a classical player, you might prefer the 3rd, 2nd, and 1st.

The koto flourish from verse two is now inserted between phrases, and a "hammer from nowhere" happens between harmonics in the 6th measure of this verse (meas. 34). Pluck the 12th-fret E-string harmonic, then quickly hammer your index finger onto the following C note and hold it while you stretch your pinky to the following B-string, 12th-fret harmonic.

The verse ends with a downward arpeggio of all harmonics; play this in the position shown for verse 1, but with the G string dampened instead of fretted.

What follows is another simulated koto glissando, played with the same kind of finger-fluttering technique that is explored in the chapter on Chinese *pipa*. If your guitar lets you reach up this high, start with your pinky on the high E string, fret 19, and your other fingers lined up as shown. You can grab a plectrum to tremolo pick this note, or do it with a fast flutter of the middle finger. Pick up your pinky to pull off to frets 15 and 13, then quickly slide down to 12.

Playing the final glissando

With all three 14-measure verses strung together, we have a faithful arrangement of a classic koto tune.

If you're hungry for more koto classics, see the book/CD *World Guitar* for an arrangement of the standard "Rokudan."

The *swarmandal* (from the Sanskrit words *swara-mandal* = "note group") is a kind of lap harp, a plucked zither that *Hindustani* singers often use to accompany themselves. (It has also been used in a very different context on a couple Beatles songs.) Traditionally, it functions in very much the same way as the strumming of drone strings on a *sitar*, filling the gaps between melody lines with glissandos and superchord-style textures. Being a fixed pitch instrument, it is always tuned to the *raga* of the music being played.

The following riffs use the same kinds of techniques that were used to cover some *koto* and sitar sounds. To get these close intervals to ring together, we can use a combination of natural harmonics and fretted notes, running down three octaves of a raga called *khamaj*, which is roughly compatible with the A Mixolydian mode. (This might bend your mind a little because when you combine harmonics and fretted notes, up and down are not what they seem to be on the guitar neck.) Pick close to the bridge to make sure the harmonics ring clearly.

Swarmandal

Raga Khamaj Exercise 1

TRACK 24

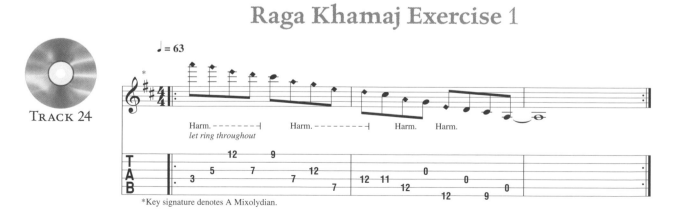

*Key signature denotes A Mixolydian.

54

Here is one that follows raga khamaj with open and fretted notes.

Raga Khamaj Exercise 2

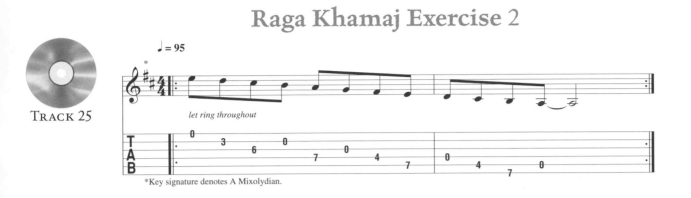

TRACK 25

*Key signature denotes A Mixolydian.

Be sure that when your fingers stretch out to reach these close intervals on adjacent strings, they are pointed straight back at the strings and the palm of your hand is not resting on the back of the neck, providing maximum clearance for all the ringing notes.

Left hand oriented to let notes ring

PERSIAN SANTUR

Ancient Iran was the birthplace of many of the world's stringed instruments. There are many hammered dulcimers in the world, including the Hungarian *cimbalom*, the Greek *santouri*, the Italian *salterio*, the Norwegian *hakkebrett*, and the list goes on. All are said to be variations on the Persian *santur*, a 2000-year-old instrument that is still played in the mysterious and complex classical music of Iran. For an introduction to the hammered dulcimer style, why not go to the source?

The santur usually has four unison strings for each note, making its sound both rich and transparent. The player "hammers" the strings with a pair of light mallets called *mezrabs*, creating smooth tremolo and quick grace notes by "bouncing" off the strings. How do you capture the multi-course timbre and percussive attack of the santur? (1) use lots of unison notes and open strings; (2) hammer!

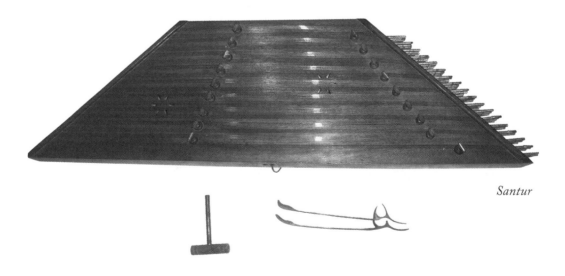

Santur

Here's an exercise to get you into the rhythmic feel of the following piece. The mezrab of choice here is a chopstick, held by the end and bounced off the strings near the soundhole. The challenge is to hit only the strings you want to sound, and dampen the others as much as possible with the fret hand.

Using a chopstick as a mallet

Chopstick "Bouncing" Exercise

"Prelude to Isfahan" is a piece composed by Morteza Neydavood, a legendary Iranian musician of the early twentieth century. The notes in this excerpt, which would usually contain quarter tones, have been adapted to suit the guitar's Western temperament.

Prelude to Isfahan
(Excerpt)

TRACK 27

LEGEND	
Tuning:	standard
Key:	E harmonic minor
Picking:	mezrab (chopstick, knitting needle, etc.)
Sound:	small-bodied steel-string acoustic

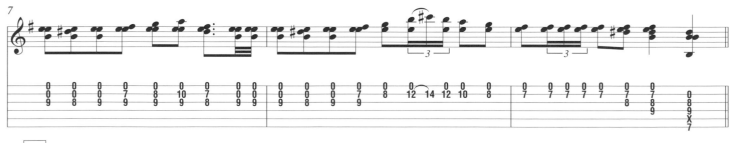

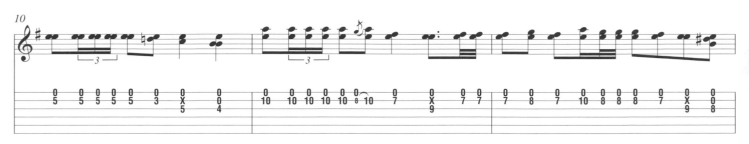

B

Prelude to Isfahan Performance Notes

This arrangement is irreverent, to say the least, but here's one concern for quality (if not authenticity): a cheap chopstick from your local takeout restaurant will not do! You need something with a smooth, finished wooden surface that bounces evenly off the strings.

When you have the right implement, work on getting a clean sound from it without any undesirable ringing notes. While you play the melody, use free fret-hand fingers and thumb to mute those unwanted strings. With a few exceptions, most of this tune is played on the high E, B, and G strings.

Mid-East Meets West

Once you have the A-section pattern down, you can start adding the decorations: quick sixteenth-note approach notes, grace-note hammer-ons, and slightly dissonant intervals (the "and" of 4, meas. 3). "Crushed" notes like these, and those to come in the B section, recreate the effect of the santur's sustaining strings that ring into each other in close intervals. They can also be a way to substitute for the quarter-tone differences between the Western temperament and Middle Eastern modes. For example, if one note of a Persian scale is somewhere in between a D♯ and an E, we might compensate by playing both the D♯ and E together—a dissonant combination. The result may not be sufficient to play a true *maqam* or *dastgah*, but it is something new that came from the meeting of two traditions.

The B section gets a bit more complex, with more dissonances and a quick trill in measure 8 that should be hammered cleanly. The second run through the B section introduces some double-striking of key notes, and a backpedaling version of the melody's upper extension: each note has its upper neighbor repeating as the melody descends.

All of these techniques and motives—distinctive trills, punctuating grace notes, and backpedaling lines—are staples in many styles of Middle Eastern music. Each tradition has its own subtleties, but the music of ancient Iran is one of the primary sources for the wealth of music that comes from the greater Middle East—and the world at large.

Keys and Metallophones

Somewhere in between the piano and drums are the solid, struck instruments with notes: xylophones, marimbas, tuned gongs, and other non-stringed melody-making instruments made of non-bendable material. We'll look at two very different varieties: the small African instrument called *mbira* and the huge Indonesian percussion ensemble called *gamelan*.

SOUTHERN AFRICAN MBIRA

The *mbira*, also known as *sanza* or *thumb piano*, is an indigenous African instrument that can be found in different forms all over the sub-Saharan region. In Zimbabwe, the *mbira dzavadzimu* is the popular instrument in the ancient music of the *Shona* people. It has at least 22 small metal keys, arranged in different registers on a sounding board and plucked with the thumbs and forefingers. Mbira music is full of polyrhythms and bouncing countermelodies, somewhat like the West African *kora* harp but with its own techniques and tonalities. Mbira players often mix three or more intertwining melodic and rhythmic parts in the same piece of music. It is at once mathematic and soulful, simple and complex, and good for the spirit.

Mbira

The guitar might seem to be a world apart from the thumb piano, but some traditional fingerpicking techniques can be readily adapted to play mbira music. A capoed, nylon-string guitar is best, as the strings are far apart for easy fingering and have a basically mellow tone. Now comes the fun part: altering your guitar to capture the sizzling sound of the mbira.

Playing with a Buzz

The mbira is built with pieces of metal or shell hanging on the keys or mounted on the body to create a buzzing sound every time a note is played. How do we recreate this on the guitar? By threading the strings with something that will vibrate along with them—in this case, staples. Use one for each string, and bend it (carefully!) around the string so that it hangs freely next to the bridge.

Staples are optional, so whether or not you've equipped your guitar for good vibrations, you can learn the following traditional Shona-style mbira vamp.

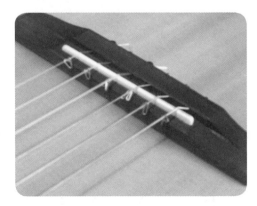

Guitar strings threaded with staples

Mbira Song

TRACK 28

LEGEND

Tuning: standard

Key: E minor (on a 10th-fret capoed guitar, the actual key is D minor)

Picking: fingers

Sound: nylon-string acoustic, capo X, strings threaded with staples

Capo X

♩. = 68

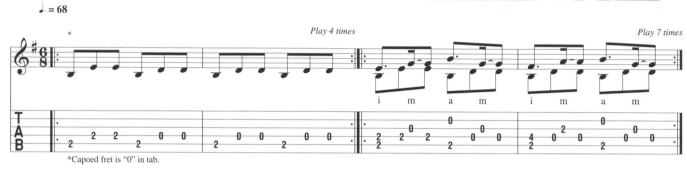

*Capoed fret is "0" in tab.

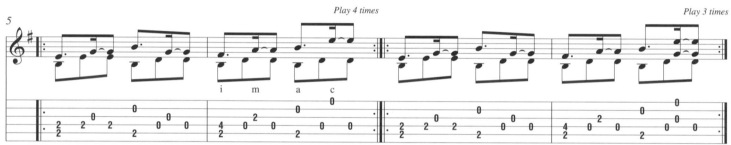

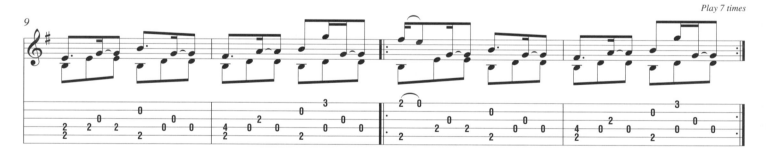

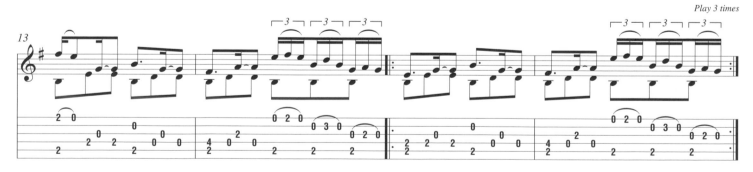

Mbira Song Performance Notes

In very African fashion, this tune establishes a busy but hypnotic vamp and adds subtle variations to it on repetitions. It is built largely on arpeggios, adding complexity as it grows. If you're playing "stapled," make sure the little buggers don't creep too far away from the bridge while you play—this could result in unwanted overtones and string muffling.

Picking and Grinning

You might be familiar with the country and western "Travis picking" technique, in which the thumb plays a bouncing bass line in 5ths while the fingers pluck a higher melody that plays off the thumb rhythmically. This can be looked at as a sort of variation on that with a different feel.

Begin with just the bass line so you can get your thumb into a groove before adding the second part and variations. If you play this part alone enough times, your thumb will just remember what to do when you introduce the picking fingers. On the fretboard, use your first finger on the A string and the second on the D string—seems pretty obvious, but your other fingers will be put to use shortly.

When you add more fingers to the next variation (meas. 3–4), notice the suggested picking pattern in the notation and think "one finger per string." Your index finger (i) picks the D string (and shares it with the thumb, picking it on the first beat of each measure), the middle finger (m) has the G string, and the ring finger (a) owns the B string. You are not obligated to use these exact fingers, but it is a good way to develop coordination. Your fret-hand pinky now gets involved on the D string, fret 4, and releases it immediately after playing (to keep the thumb groove going).

Pinky finger reaching over to play D string

Again, repeat this pattern until you are comfortable grooving with it. Repetition is the best way to learn finger independence. Play it slowly, over and over, until you fall asleep or your neighbors start complaining. When you're ready to bring it up to speed, you must put faith in your fingers; they will know where to go! Let your mind wander to Zimbabwe (unless you already happen to be there).

You could do this all day and be entranced and content, but sheer repetition isn't enough. Besides, your pick-hand pinky (c) deserves to get involved. Use it, if you choose, to pluck the high-E string and add another layer of variety to the pattern. The old school of classical guitar neglects this useful finger unless it's absolutely necessary. Now is your chance to get all of your digits involved and coordinated! The following section brings the high-E and G strings together for more texture.

But Wait, There's More!

Your fret-hand ring finger, which hasn't been involved yet, is useful for the next layer of melody: a high-G and F# pulled off to E. (Notice that in the notation, this is added as a third part on top of the other two.) Use the same finger to fret both notes (the others are spoken for) and pull it downward to snap the string to an open (capoed) position. This adds a second melody to the mix and might confuse your fingers again. Feel free to slow it way down and repeat *ad infinitum* for practice.

Having built the vamp with ever-increasing complexity, we can get a little flashy with the next variation, using a group of *hammered* and *pulled triplets*. The bass line necessarily simplifies when this happens, as you're now using the first and second fingers to hammer and pull. Hammer-ons and pull-offs are not exactly mbira techniques but they are a very guitar-friendly way to "fake it." The mbira player plucks every note on runs like this!

A final variation, simply adding the high-E string to another part of the main melody, brings it home to rest.

Practice Tip: Tap It!

On top of pure repetition, there's another way to develop your picking fingers on a complex pattern like this when your guitar isn't nearby: simply tap out the picking pattern with your fingers on a desk, dashboard, table, or your knee. Tap once for every pluck on the guitar, and use the correct fingerpicking pattern, adding your pinky whenever it's called for. You might irritate your friends and co-workers, but they might just appreciate your rhythm.

INDONESIAN GAMELAN

The mostly percussion orchestras of Indonesia, consisting mainly of bronze xylophone- and gong-type metallophone instruments (but also drums, flutes, zithers, voices, etc.), are called *gamelan*. There are different varieties of gamelan in different regions and performance settings, including the smaller, dynamic and energetic Balinese ensembles and the full-blown classical gamelan of central Java. We'll take a look at one example from the Javanese repertoire which uses intertwining melodies and counter-rhythms (in a seven-note scale called *pelog*, one of two major Javanese tonalities) to create highly structured music that is both textural and complex, energizing and serene.

Gamelan ensemble

"Bubaran Hudan Mas" is a good "light" introduction to the relatively heavy world of gamelan music. It is a short piece traditionally played at the end of a concert or play while the audience files out, and, unlike most gamelan pieces, it has essentially one repeated section. In this arrangement, the *balungan* ("skeleton"), or central melody, is played in "straight" quarter notes—notated as eighths, because a composite part of higher melodic embellishments plays counterpoint to the balungan. The lower gong part is notated separately at the bottom of the staves for clarity.

This is a somewhat skeletal arrangement of a piece that would have many more elements to it, some playing in unison and others in variation. Suffice it to say that the balungan and lower gong parts are true to form, while the upper counter-melody is like a thumbnail sketch of a much larger work. This arrangement has also been adjusted to a Western temperament (the Javanese system uses some quarter-tone intervals).

Bubaran Hudan Mas

TRACK 29

LEGEND

Tuning: standard

Tonality: variation of B pelog (on a 10th-fret capoed guitar, the actual key is A): B–C–D–(E)–F–G

Picking: fingerstyle

Sound: steel-string acoustic, capo X

Capo X

Relaxed ♩ = 120

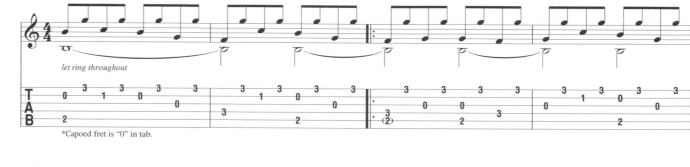

let ring throughout

*Capoed fret is "0" in tab.

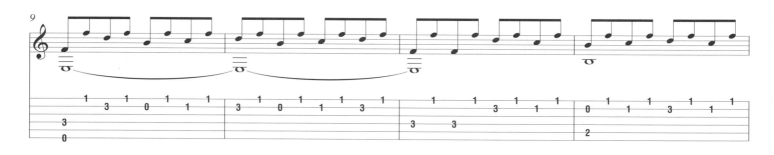

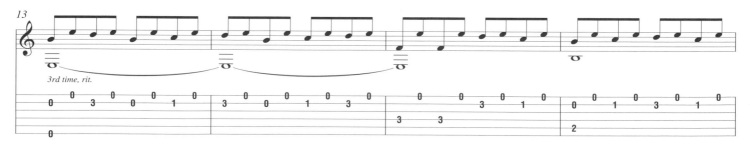

3rd time, rit.

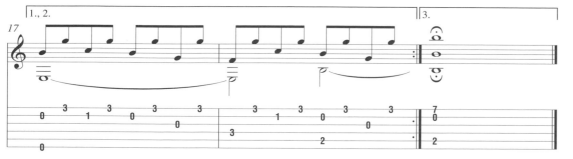

Bubaran Hudan Mas Performance Notes

Sizzling Intervals

You might notice a little dissonance in this tune. In our capoed reality, E and F notes regularly mingle with the melody and its lower and upper variants, made even more crunchy with a B note (the #4 of F, or the *tritone*, a.k.a. "the Devil's interval"). The intermittent vibrating effect that results from such dissonance is desired in Javanese gamelan music. (In the Balinese tradition, pairs of instruments are deliberately tuned a quarter-tone "off" from each other for extra sizzle.)

You can keep your fretting fingers in relatively the same position throughout this piece: middle finger on the A string, fret 2 (relative to the capo); ring finger on fret 3 of the D string; and your index and pinky fingers hovering around frets 1 and 3 (respectively) on the B and high-E strings. The index finger will have to quickly cover the B and high-E strings in a mini-barre at measure 9, on the "and" of 2 and beat 4.

Main playing position

There is a highly nuanced organization in gamelan music, based on cycles and convergences; we can see some examples of that here. The lower gong part hits a B note intermittently, most importantly at times when the main melody also lands on B. The same B note appears on beat 1 at the start of the piece and doesn't land on beat 1 again until the end, after a slowdown that cues all instruments to close on B. Imagine that these countermelodies represent planets rotating around the sun at different rates and converging at key moments—that's a snapshot of the gamelan experience.

SOURCE RECORDINGS AND RECOMMENDED MEDIA

Raíces Latinas: Smithsonian Folkways Latino Roots Collection. (CD) SFW CD 40470

Mishka (website of Russian traditional music) – www.mishka.com

Barynya (Russian music ensemble) – www.barynya.com

Bonnie Wade, *Music in India: The Classical Traditions* (book) Manohar ISBN 81-85054-25-8

Various Artists, *Exotic Strings*. (CD) ARC Records EUCD 1823

Lui Pui-Yuen, China: *Music of the Pipa*. (CD) Nonesuch Explorer Series 9 72085-2

Tsugaru Shamisen: The World of Michihiro Sato. (DVD) IMC Music IMM 940097

Aiko Hasegawa, *The Art of the Japanese Koto*. ARC Records EUCD 1907

The Griot (film) – www.thegriotmovie.com

Lamin Saho (Kora Player and Griot from Gambia) – www.laminsaho.tk

Various Artists, *Persian Music – A Century of Santur*. (CD) Mahoor Institute of Culture and Art, 2007.

Zimbabwe: The African Mbira: Music of the Shona People. (CD) Nonesuch Explorer Series 79703-2

Java: Javanese Court Gamelan. (CD) Nonesuch Explorer Series 9 72044-2

Greg Herriges, *World Guitar*. (book/CD) Hal Leonard Corporation HL00695824

Julie Lyonn Lieberman, *Planet Musician*. (book/CD) Hal Leonard Corporation HL00220008

GUITAR NOTATION LEGEND

Guitar music can be notated three different ways: on a *musical staff*, in *tablature*, and in *rhythm slashes*.

RHYTHM SLASHES are written above the staff. Strum chords in the rhythm indicated. Use the chord diagrams found at the top of the first page of the transcription for the appropriate chord voicings. Round noteheads indicate single notes.

THE MUSICAL STAFF shows pitches and rhythms and is divided by bar lines into measures. Pitches are named after the first seven letters of the alphabet.

TABLATURE graphically represents the guitar fingerboard. Each horizontal line represents a string, and each number represents a fret.

4th string, 2nd fret | 1st & 2nd strings open, played together | open D chord

DEFINITIONS FOR SPECIAL GUITAR NOTATION

HALF-STEP BEND: Strike the note and bend up 1/2 step.

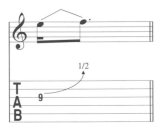

WHOLE-STEP BEND: Strike the note and bend up one step.

GRACE NOTE BEND: Strike the note and immediately bend up as indicated.

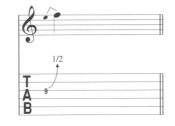

SLIGHT (MICROTONE) BEND: Strike the note and bend up 1/4 step.

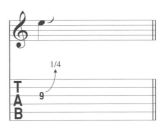

BEND AND RELEASE: Strike the note and bend up as indicated, then release back to the original note. Only the first note is struck.

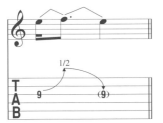

PRE-BEND: Bend the note as indicated, then strike it.

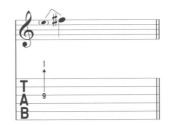

PRE-BEND AND RELEASE: Bend the note as indicated. Strike it and release the bend back to the original note.

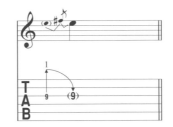

UNISON BEND: Strike the two notes simultaneously and bend the lower note up to the pitch of the higher.

VIBRATO: The string is vibrated by rapidly bending and releasing the note with the fretting hand.

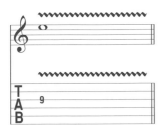

WIDE VIBRATO: The pitch is varied to a greater degree by vibrating with the fretting hand.

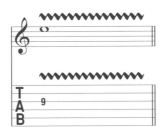

HAMMER-ON: Strike the first (lower) note with one finger, then sound the higher note (on the same string) with another finger by fretting it without picking.

PULL-OFF: Place both fingers on the notes to be sounded. Strike the first note and without picking, pull the finger off to sound the second (lower) note.

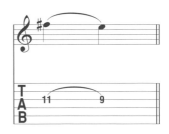

LEGATO SLIDE: Strike the first note and then slide the same fret-hand finger up or down to the second note. The second note is not struck.

SHIFT SLIDE: Same as legato slide, except the second note is struck.

TRILL: Very rapidly alternate between the notes indicated by continuously hammering on and pulling off.

TAPPING: Hammer ("tap") the fret indicated with the pick-hand index or middle finger and pull off to the note fretted by the fret hand.

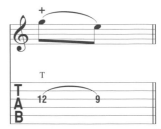

NATURAL HARMONIC: Strike the note while the fret-hand lightly touches the string directly over the fret indicated.

PINCH HARMONIC: The note is fretted normally and a harmonic is produced by adding the edge of the thumb or the tip of the index finger of the pick hand to the normal pick attack.

HARP HARMONIC: The note is fretted normally and a harmonic is produced by gently resting the pick hand's index finger directly above the indicated fret (in parentheses) while the pick hand's thumb or pick assists by plucking the appropriate string.

PICK SCRAPE: The edge of the pick is rubbed down (or up) the string, producing a scratchy sound.

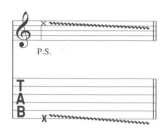

MUFFLED STRINGS: A percussive sound is produced by laying the fret hand across the string(s) without depressing, and striking them with the pick hand.

PALM MUTING: The note is partially muted by the pick hand lightly touching the string(s) just before the bridge.

RAKE: Drag the pick across the strings indicated with a single motion.

TREMOLO PICKING: The note is picked as rapidly and continuously as possible.

ARPEGGIATE: Play the notes of the chord indicated by quickly rolling them from bottom to top.

VIBRATO BAR DIVE AND RETURN: The pitch of the note or chord is dropped a specified number of steps (in rhythm), then returned to the original pitch.

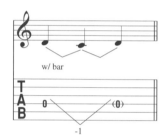

VIBRATO BAR SCOOP: Depress the bar just before striking the note, then quickly release the bar.

VIBRATO BAR DIP: Strike the note and then immediately drop a specified number of steps, then release back to the original pitch.

ADDITIONAL MUSICAL DEFINITIONS

(accent)	• Accentuate note (play it louder).
(accent)	• Accentuate note with great intensity.
(staccato)	• Play the note short.
⊓	• Downstroke
V	• Upstroke
D.S. al Coda	• Go back to the sign (%), then play until the measure marked "*To Coda*," then skip to the section labelled "**Coda**."
D.C. al Fine	• Go back to the beginning of the song and play until the measure marked "*Fine*" (end).

Rhy. Fig.	• Label used to recall a recurring accompaniment pattern (usually chordal).
Riff	• Label used to recall composed, melodic lines (usually single notes) which recur.
Fill	• Label used to identify a brief melodic figure which is to be inserted into the arrangement.
Rhy. Fill	• A chordal version of a Fill.
tacet	• Instrument is silent (drops out).
	• Repeat measures between signs.
	• When a repeated section has different endings, play the first ending only the first time and the second ending only the second time.

NOTE: Tablature numbers in parentheses mean:
    1. The note is being sustained over a system (note in standard notation is tied), or
    2. The note is sustained, but a new articulation (such as a hammer-on, pull-off, slide or vibrato) begins, or
    3. The note is a barely audible "ghost" note (note in standard notation is also in parentheses).

ABOUT THE AUTHOR

Guitarist, multi-instrumentalist, author, and award-winning composer, Greg Herriges' writing for Hal Leonard Corporation includes the book/CD *World Guitar*, many books in the *Guitar Songs for Dummies* series, and contributions to *Guitar Edge* magazine. With a foundation in progressive rock and fingerstyle acoustic guitar, Greg immersed himself in the study of Ethnomusicology, specializing in South and East Asian art music with a focus on Javanese gamelan and Hindustani classical music. A 2009 winner of the Bush Foundation Artist Fellowship for Music Composition, he performs solo and with cross-cultural ensembles, composes and directs music for theatre and film, and shares his discoveries in workshops and lessons. Greg's CDs of original and traditional world music include *It Plays Me* and *Telluric Currents*. More musical discoveries can be found at www.gregherriges.com.

Get Better at Guitar

...with these Great Guitar Instruction Books from Hal Leonard!

101 GUITAR TIPS
STUFF ALL THE PROS KNOW AND USE
by Adam St. James

This book contains invaluable guidance on everything from scales and music theory to truss rod adjustments, proper recording studio set-ups, and much more. The book also features snippets of advice from some of the most celebrated guitarists and producers in the music business, including B.B. King, Steve Vai, Joe Satriani, Warren Haynes, Laurence Juber, Pete Anderson, Tom Dowd and others, culled from the author's hundreds of interviews.
00695737 Book/CD Pack..........................$16.95

AMAZING PHRASING
50 WAYS TO IMPROVE YOUR IMPROVISATIONAL SKILLS
by Tom Kolb

This book/CD pack explores all the main components necessary for crafting well-balanced rhythmic and melodic phrases. It also explains how these phrases are put together to form cohesive solos. Many styles are covered – rock, blues, jazz, fusion, country, Latin, funk and more – and all of the concepts are backed up with musical examples. The companion CD contains 89 demos for listening, and most tracks feature full-band backing.
00695583 Book/CD Pack..........................$19.95

BLUES YOU CAN USE
by John Ganapes

A comprehensive source designed to help guitarists develop both lead and rhythm playing. Covers: Texas, Delta, R&B, early rock and roll, gospel, blues/rock and more. Includes: 21 complete solos • chord progressions and riffs • turnarounds • moveable scales and more. CD features leads and full band backing.
00695007 Book/CD Pack..........................$19.95

FRETBOARD MASTERY
by Troy Stetina

Untangle the mysterious regions of the guitar fretboard and unlock your potential. *Fretboard Mastery* familiarizes you with all the shapes you need to know by applying them in real musical examples, thereby reinforcing and reaffirming your newfound knowledge. The result is a much higher level of comprehension and retention.
00695331 Book/CD Pack..........................$19.95

FRETBOARD ROADMAPS – 2ND EDITION
ESSENTIAL GUITAR PATTERNS THAT ALL THE PROS KNOW AND USE
by Fred Sokolow

The updated edition of this bestseller features more songs, updated lessons, and a full audio CD! Learn to play lead and rhythm anywhere on the fretboard, in any key; play a variety of lead guitar styles; play chords and progressions anywhere on the fretboard; expand your chord vocabulary; and learn to think musically – the way the pros do.
00695941 Book/CD Pack..........................$14.95

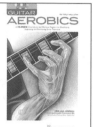

GUITAR AEROBICS
A 52-WEEK, ONE-LICK-PER-DAY WORKOUT PROGRAM FOR DEVELOPING, IMPROVING & MAINTAINING GUITAR TECHNIQUE
by Troy Nelson

From the former editor of *Guitar One* magazine, here is a daily dose of vitamins to keep your chops fine tuned! Musical styles include rock, blues, jazz, metal, country, and funk. Techniques taught include alternate picking, arpeggios, sweep picking, string skipping, legato, string bending, and rhythm guitar. These exercises will increase speed, and improve dexterity and pick- and fret-hand accuracy. The accompanying CD includes all 365 workout licks plus play-along grooves in every style at eight different metronome settings.
00695946 Book/CD Pack..........................$19.95

GUITAR CLUES
OPERATION PENTATONIC
by Greg Koch

Join renowned guitar master Greg Koch as he clues you in to a wide variety of fun and valuable pentatonic scale applications. Whether you're new to improvising or have been doing it for a while, this book/CD pack will provide loads of delicious licks and tricks that you can use right away, from volume swells and chicken pickin' to intervallic and chordal ideas. The CD includes 65 demo and play-along tracks.
00695827 Book/CD Pack..........................$19.95

INTRODUCTION TO GUITAR TONE & EFFECTS
by David M. Brewster

This book/CD pack teaches the basics of guitar tones and effects, with audio examples on CD. Readers will learn about: overdrive, distortion and fuzz • using equalizers • modulation effects • reverb and delay • multi-effect processors • and more.
00695766 Book/CD Pack..........................$14.95

PICTURE CHORD ENCYCLOPEDIA

This comprehensive guitar chord resource for all playing styles and levels features five voicings of 44 chord qualities for all twelve keys – 2,640 chords in all! For each, there is a clearly illustrated chord frame, as well as *an actual photo* of the chord being played! Includes info on basic fingering principles, open chords and barre chords, partial chords and broken-set forms, and more.
00695224 ....$19.95

SCALE CHORD RELATIONSHIPS
by Michael Mueller & Jeff Schroedl

This book teaches players how to determine which scales to play with which chords, so guitarists will never have to fear chord changes again! This book/CD pack explains how to: recognize keys • analyze chord progressions • use the modes • play over nondiatonic harmony • use harmonic and melodic minor scales • use symmetrical scales such as chromatic, whole-tone and diminished scales • incorporate exotic scales such as Hungarian major and Gypsy minor • and much more!
00695563 Book/CD Pack..........................$14.95

SPEED MECHANICS FOR LEAD GUITAR

Take your playing to the stratosphere with the most advanced lead book by this proven heavy metal author. *Speed Mechanics* is the ultimate technique book for developing the kind of speed and precision in today's explosive playing styles. Learn the fastest ways to achieve speed and control, secrets to make your practice time really count, and how to open your ears and make your musical ideas more solid and tangible. Packed with over 200 vicious exercises including Troy's scorching version of "Flight of the Bumblebee." Music and examples demonstrated on CD. 89-minute audio.
00699323 Book/CD Pack..........................$19.95

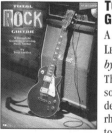

TOTAL ROCK GUITAR
A COMPLETE GUIDE TO LEARNING ROCK GUITAR
by Troy Stetina

This unique and comprehensive source for learning rock guitar is designed to develop both lead and rhythm playing. It covers: getting a tone that rocks • open chords, power chords and barre chords • riffs, scales and licks • string bending, strumming, palm muting, harmonics and alternate picking • all rock styles • and much more. The examples are in standard notation with chord grids and tab, and the CD includes full-band backing for all 22 songs.
00695246 Book/CD Pack..........................$19.99